PRAISE FOR On Becoming an Artist

"Ellen Langer, clearly one of the most creative people around today, has written another groundbreaking book showing through research and her own experience how and why pursuing mindful creativity may lead to the artful life we all desire. Its wit and charm will appeal to everyone."

—DEEPAK CHOPRA, author of *The Seven Spiritual Laws of Success*

"Whether painting, writing, or just being, Dr. Langer, a renaissance woman, offers profound insights into how and why to increase our mindful creativity."

—BETTY FRIEDAN

"The unconventional originality of Ellen Langer's mind wakes up those of us who, for fear of failure, do not dare to 'just do it.' Her most provocative book opens for thousands of us a prospect, like Ellen, of becoming an artist."

—R. B. ZAJONC, Stanford University

"Without making extravagant promises about releasing our inner Michelangelos, *On Becoming an Artist* is provocative, liberating, and in itself a significant act of mindful creativity."

—JUSTIN KAPLAN, Pulitzer Prize–winning author of *Mr. Clemens and Mark Twain*

"*On Becoming an Artist* is a wise and most original book. Ellen Langer's innovative study of why and how people let roadblocks stand in the way of meaningful creativity is a pleasure to read. With its keen insight into how mindlessness can be costly and mindful creativity can help people live more meaningful lives, it is a must read, especially for people who want to change their lives but haven't quite been able to."

—ELIZABETH LOFTUS, distinguished professor, University of California-Irvine

Also by Ellen J. Langer

Mindfulness
The Power of Mindful Learning

On Becoming an Artist

Ballantine Books　New York

On Becoming an

Artist

Reinventing Yourself
Through Mindful Creativity

ELLEN J. LANGER

2006 Ballantine Books Trade Paperback Edition

Copyright © 2005 Ellen Langer, Ph.d.

Originally published in hardcover in the United States
by Ballantine Books, an imprint of The Random House Publishing Group,
a division of Random House, Inc., in 2005.

Grateful acknowledgment is made to New Directions Publishing Corp.
for permission to reprint "This Is Just to Say" by William Carlos Williams
from *Collected Poems: 1909–1939, Volume I,* copyright © 1938
by New Directions Publishing Corp. Reprinted by permission
of New Directions Publishing Corp.

Library of Congress Cataloging-in-Publication Data

Langer, Ellen J.
On becoming an artist : reinventing yourself
through mindful creativity / Ellen J. Langer.—1st ed.
p.   cm.
Includes bibliographical references and index.
ISBN 0-345-45630-0 (trade pbk.)
1. Creative ability.   2. Attention.   I. Title.

BF408.L36 2005
153.3'5—dc22   2004057654

Book design by Simon M. Sullivan

Printed in the United States of America

2   4   6   8   9   7   5   3   1

For Norman, always supportive and loving.

Contents

Acknowledgments

THERE ARE MANY PEOPLE TO WHOM I OWE GRATITUDE FOR THEIR help on various aspects of this book. There are those who helped me with the art of painting, those who helped me with the art of writing, and those who have contributed to my endless pursuit of the art of living. With respect to my art, I want especially to thank Anthony Russo for sharing his wisdom, support, and friendship from the beginning of this adventure to the present. Sophia Snow, Barbara Cohen, and Del Felardi were also very helpful with their insights, support, and candor. I'm grateful to Elaine Noble, Merloyd Lawrence, Marion Roth, Richard Beckwith, John Frank, Julie Heller, Jan Kelley, Linda Russo, and the woman in the hardware store on Conwell Street in Provincetown, each of whom is probably unaware of how he or she encouraged me in this pursuit. Rhoda Rossmore, by contrast, could not be unaware of her strong influence because she has been there from the beginning and has seen virtually each of my early paintings in various stages of completion.

Mike Moldoveneau and Pamela Painter, both in their own ways, played a very important part in helping me write this book. Michele Leichtman, Eric Rofes, and Phyllis Katz also gave me many useful comments on various drafts that helped me to clarify my thoughts both for myself and for the reader. I also want to express my sincere gratitude to my editor, Nancy Miller, for her support and encouragement for my work and my art and for putting the final brushstrokes on this book.

Writing requires that someone have something to write about. I am first a social psychologist. The social psychological research that my student collaborators and I conducted provides the evidence on which this book is largely based. Therefore, I want to thank Tal Ben-Schachar, David Borden, Shauna Campbell, Leslie Coates-Burpee, Matt Cohen, Brianna Cummings, Laura Delizonna, Noah Eisenkraft, Brianna Ewert, Emily Falk, Allan Filipowicz, Sarit Golub, Adam Grant, Brett Hemenway, Megan Kovak, Greg Kulessa, Amanda Mulfinger, Jesse Preston, Wendy Smith, Nikko Sommaripa, and Yulia Steshenko for their help with the many research projects described in this book. It is difficult to conduct research with special populations without the help of generous people who gain little except the pursuit of knowledge. I am very grateful to Alejandro Gomez Rubio, who runs the Dolphin Center in Puerto Vallarta, Mexico; to Kathy Streeker, who runs the New England Aquarium; and to Ellen Ventura, who owns Van Elgers dog boarding in Dartmouth, Massachusetts.

David Miller, my agent, editor, art critic, and most important, dear friend, has been the most essential person from the beginning to the end of this project. Among other things, it was he who managed to help me integrate what may have seemed at times to be at least two separate books into what finally became *On Becoming an Artist.* Our trips to museums and wonderful discussions about art and life are very precious to me.

Finally I want to acknowledge Nancy Hemenway, who is the single most significant person to my successful engagement in all phases of this book. It is to her that I turned to see if the ideas were meaningful, whether I should keep or delete any particular written material, and if I should add more detail or color to each of my paintings. I owe her dearly, not just for all the fancy brushes, paints, and canvases she gave me but for giving me a new passion for my lifetime.

Introduction

ALL IT TAKES TO BECOME AN ARTIST IS TO START DOING ART.

I spend my summers on Cape Cod, and as each June approaches, I'm reminded how lucky I am to be an academic and have some time off from teaching. At the beginning of the summer the plan is always the same: play tennis in the morning, have lunch with friends, and then write in the afternoon before breaking for the evening's activities. Rarely do I come close to following this plan, but one summer I deviated not only from the plan but from anything I might have imagined previously.

It had been raining almost nonstop all week when I ran into an artist friend, Jane Winters, in town. She asked what the day held for me, and to my surprise I said I was thinking of taking up painting. I have no idea why I said that. I don't think I'd had more than a fleeting thought or two about painting in my entire life up to that point. Yet Jane not only encouraged me to paint but insisted we go to her studio so she could give me some small canvases to start me on my way. I said one would be enough, but she insisted that I take five. "Your first painting shouldn't be too precious," she said, warning me of the critiques I'd soon face.

Coincidentally, later that afternoon I had to deliver something to another artist friend, Cy Fried. His wife, Miriam, is also a painter, and while I was at their house I mentioned to her that I was thinking of taking up painting. (It had become my what-do-you-say-to-a-painter-when-you-don't-know-what-else-to-say response.) She replied, "That's great. Now get yourself a large canvas and just do it. Don't evaluate your work. Just do it." Except for the size of the canvas, Jane's and Miriam's advice had been the same: Don't let judgments get in your way.

A week or so later, I did my first painting on a small wooden shingle I had found. The painting was of a girl on a horse, racing through the woods. I was surprised at how much I liked it. I was afraid to show it to anybody, yet at the same time I felt compelled to find out if someone—anyone—thought it was any good. I decided to show it to the woman in the art supply store in Provincetown where I had bought my first tubes of paint. She didn't know me, and I thought with my clinical skills as a psychologist I'd be able to decode her reaction if she pretended to like it. I don't remember exactly what she said when I showed her the painting, but I do remember feeling that she genuinely appreciated it. I know now that no matter what she had said, I'd had enormous fun painting and I knew I didn't want to stop. So I didn't.

I moved from painting on shingles to painting on canvases. My first attempt on a canvas was a horse that appeared to be gleefully kicking his back heels together. I loved looking at my horse painting, so I painted another, and another, and another. I painted a horse calmly standing on both sides of a fence at the same time, oblivious to his being in this "impossible" position. I was completely engaged in what I was doing. I loved every minute of painting; then I loved trying to figure out why I painted what I painted.

A close friend saw my first creation—my painting of the girl on horseback—and commented, "They're never as good as the first one." I don't think she meant to be unsupportive; in fact, I took it to mean that she liked my first painting. I have since come to see why the first creation might actually be the best, if the paintings that follow are indeed more scripted. It is because with the first one is engaged mindfully. I was fully present when I painted the girl on horseback, did not evaluate it while I painted it, didn't mindlessly follow any rules—I couldn't because I didn't know any.

In my two previous books, *Mindfulness* and *The Power of Mindful Learning,* I compare mindlessness with the unconscious and discuss how rampant and costly living a life mindlessly can be. In traditional notions of the unconscious, we do not see certain things because we are motivated not to—to do so would be too painful for us. Mindlessness, instead, typically comes about by default, not design. When we live our lives mindlessly, we don't see, hear, taste, or experience much of what might turn lives verging on boredom into lives that are rich and exciting. We are essentially "not there" to notice much of the world around us. Beginning an artistic activity is one way to help us move from excessive mindlessness to a more mindful life. If we fully engage this new activity, we will come to see how enlivening mindfulness is. Aware of the phenomenological experience of mindfulness, we can let an internal bell sound whenever we feel otherwise, signaling that mindlessness is creeping in.

That all sounds well and good, but as much as we'd like to try this new activity, most of us are afraid to begin. Many of us have neglected beginning new creative activities like painting, art, music, or sports as we pursued careers and families, thinking we'd get to those creative activities later. As much as we might want to try, we keep putting them off because we're afraid of making fools of ourselves as we take up new activities for the first time. I experienced these feelings as I continued doing art.

I found that it was surprisingly hard not to worry about what others would think of my art. There is an artist in town whose painting of a horse hung in a gallery window. I couldn't help but compare one of my horse pictures with hers, which was very good and very pricey. Her canvas was very large and mine small; her horse was thin, bent down, and interestingly horse-like. Mine was paunchy, bent down, and kind of whimsical. Hers was mostly purple and mine lime green. I didn't know if any of these were differences that mattered. I began to ask others what they thought about our two pictures; I was trying to find out what I should do if I wanted to become a better painter. Apparently I wasn't the only one who was interested in comparing our paintings. Three times I was asked, "Did you see the horse at the gallery on Commercial Street? Yours reminds me of hers." Another artist friend said she preferred my horse. I couldn't believe it. I was thrilled. I still didn't know the underlying ways in which the two horse paintings were different, or why some people preferred one over the other, but now I had more courage to try to find out.

I asked in the gallery about the artist and was told she was a "serious" woman. After some thought, it appeared to me that the people who preferred my horse painting seemed to be "happier" rather than "serious" people, for lack of a single more appropriate term. Any difference between the two paintings in this respect was very subtle, though; neither horse is smiling or frowning. I began to wonder about the relationship between one's consciousness and one's preferences. How much of one's mindfulness could be transferred to the canvas?

I remember visiting a friend, Phyllis Katz, in New York, several years before I began painting. Phyllis's apartment is filled with beautiful things, and the space itself is large and dramatic.

The walls were covered with spectacular and in some instances very unusual art. The night I was visiting, Phyllis was having a board meeting for a psychological organization. Although her apartment was starting to fill up with psychologists, I insisted that she watch a very short video I had just taken of my foal only minutes old; I was too excited to wait until the meeting ended. Alone in the den, I loaded the video on her latest equipment and pressed all the buttons in front of me because I had no idea which one would start it. The video began, and the foal's every move was sweetly narrated. One of the buttons I had accidentally pressed piped the narration through speakers around the apartment. Outside the den, the psychologists assumed it was part of an "art show" and walked around looking at Phyllis's unusual art while listening to a voice narrating the foal's birth.

I heard the psychologists discussing the "show" after the video was done. The discussion was fascinating, as they made sense of the art through the ideas about birth and entering the world on one's feet, as only a horse could do, expressed in the audio portion of my video.

These experiences convinced me that whatever we engage with becomes engaging, whether or not someone "official" calls it art. If we put evaluation aside, the world almost instantly becomes more available for mindful viewing. If we stop judging ourselves, creating art becomes more possible. The difficulty lies in convincing ourselves to refrain from judgment. A student friend, Sophia Snow, visited me on the Cape and we painted together. Sophia had been good at art as a child, and I expressed some concern about my work not being nearly as good as hers. She reminded me of what I had taught in my Harvard class: that evaluations are dependent on context, and that making both good and bad judgments can be mindless.

It may also be easier to put evaluation aside once we realize that most of the paintings we see in museums were rejected in their day. In 1863, an important juried show refused thousands of paintings that were submitted, including Édouard Manet's important painting *Déjeuner sur l'herbe,* which depicted a modern woman instead of the more typical nymph in a classical scene. Rather than recognize *Déjeuner sur l'herbe* for what it was, "those in the know" criticized Manet for not conforming to their traditional notions of art, describing the painting as anti-academic and vulgar. The content of the painting may have been what set the critics to attack Manet's technical choices. His choice of harsh lighting and the "elimination of midtones" upset the academy. And yet it was *Déjeuner sur l'herbe* and Manet's next painting, *Olympia,* that defined the beginning of Impressionism. There is a similar story to be told for each new movement in art. People don't give up their current preferences or ideas easily.

I put aside painting horses and moved on to scenes with people in them. The psychological significance for me was overwhelming. I painted my dear friend Nancy and me in chairs by the windows—my first painting that had "real" content. The chairs were right there in front of me. I set out to paint the two of us sitting where we often sat, reading and enjoying the morning. When I stepped back to look at the painting, I was amazed. True to form, the floor was slanted toward her, she was trying to read, and I was busy talking to her, book in hand but my attention elsewhere.

I am still surprised by the psychological significance of my paintings. One night I called my friend Elaine right before I went to bed. She said she had just stepped out of the shower, and I told her I was envious that she had had a relaxing shower to end the day. Not surprisingly she said, "So get up and take a shower." As nice a thought as it was, though, I had already called the day over, and so I went to sleep. The next morning I arose at six and started painting almost immediately. I painted mindfully, loving every minute, unscripted and unaware of whatever rules trained artists might say I should be following. I stepped back from the canvas when it was nearly complete and found a painting of a woman who had just finished a painting of a man who needed a shave taking a bath with a cigarette dangling from his mouth. Although I was unaware of this at the time, he represented to me the epitome of someone in need of a bath. I put the brush down, went into the bathroom, and turned the bathwater on. Whether the painting represented anything meaningful or not, I couldn't be sure. But I was sure that a mindful analysis of it after the fact made me want to take a bath.

Although this book is more personal than *Mindfulness* and *The Power of Mindful Creativity*, the professional reader will notice that much accepted wisdom of the field is questioned and alternative concepts are offered, just as in those books. This is especially true regarding social comparison theory, theories of talent, and decision-making theory.

Mindful creativity has enriched and enhanced my life. My enthusiasm for painting and a mindful analysis of my work persists, and the fun this mindful engagement with the canvas brings me continues. Most important—as I hope *On Becoming an Artist* will show—leading a more mindful and rewarding life is readily available to anyone who can put evaluation aside and just engage in new, creative endeavors.

On Becoming an Artist

I

A Life of Mindful Creativity

*What attracted me was less art itself than the artist's life and all that it
meant for me: the idea of creativity and freedom of expression and
action. I had been attracted to painting and drawing for a long time,
but it was not an irresistible passion; what I wanted, at all costs, was to
escape the monotony of life.*

PIERRE BONNARD

ALL OF US HAVE HAD THE EXPERIENCE OF BEING TOTALLY ENGAGED
in something—a movie, an afternoon of adventure, or a new
love affair—and, like Bonnard, we seek lives steeped in such experiences. Bonnard found creative engagement in painting and
lived a rich life that many dream of and most consider the realm
of only a few special, talented people. That belief, however, is
wrong. Complete, creative engagement in all that we do is the
natural response to our world; it need not be extraordinary at
all. It is, in fact, the experience we have when we are at play.
Whether it's at play or in a more serious pursuit, if we approach
the opportunity at hand creatively, we will experience such engagement. In the best of all worlds, a life of total engagement
would be the norm, although in reality too many of us don't see
the opportunity before us. What's more, we seem to do everything possible to prevent it from happening.

Too much of the time, we are not seeing, hearing, tasting, or
experiencing what would turn lives troubled by boredom and

loneliness into lives that are rich and exciting. We unwittingly give up our potential for creative endeavor and in the process live sealed in unlived lives, where monotony is the rule rather than the exception. Creativity is not a blessing some special few are born with or receive from above. Our creative nature is an integral part of our daily lives, expressed through our culture, our language, and even our most mundane activities. "Art," wrote the painter Robert Henri, "when really understood is the province of every human being."

This book is about the roadblocks that stand in the way of our natural creativity. It is intended to be a guide to opening up to creative engagement on a daily basis in all that we do. Imagine being very hungry and wandering into a room with a table full of delicious food. If the room were empty of people, none of us would need any extra motivation. We would taste some of everything, eat what we liked, and enjoy the feast. But fill the room with people and we would face a host of concerns that would give us pause: how the others might judge us if we filled our plates; whether we shouldn't, given the circumstances, watch our weight instead of eating heartily; or whether to listen to the judgments of others about the merits of a particular dish. Faced with such socially induced concerns, we might well remain hungry. In the same way, there are socially constructed roadblocks that keep us from experiencing our creative selves. While some may argue that it is a good thing to learn to curb our appetite at times, I don't think any would argue that it is to our benefit to forgo the pleasure of our natural creativity.

Engaging our creativity more fully, giving it a form that holds some innate interest, ought be part of everyday life for each of us. How often have we neglected activities like art, music, writing, dance—or a host of other creative endeavors—as we pursue careers and families? We might regretfully add them to the list of things we'll get to later, but we think little about why we are doing so. Then one day we realize that now is yesterday's later. We typically regard such creative pursuits as "leisure" activities, and that word suggests they are rather unimportant. They may well, however, hold the key to the problem of finding meaning and fulfillment in the rest of our lives. Because we take them to be for our "leisure," they need not carry the threat to our self-esteem that changes in other aspects of our lives do.

Unfortunately, our culture leads us to evaluate almost everything we do, even our works of art, music, literature, and every other creative product. We look at the end product and pass judgment on whether it is "creative" or not without regard for whether a mindfully engaged individual created it. We distinguish the product from the experience of creating it. For most of us, it is a terrifying prospect to imagine being judged in this way. If we could put aside our concern for others' judgment of the product, however, creative engagement could transform our lives through whatever creative endeavors we might choose. We can learn to choose to engage creatively in any number of ways, simply by learning how to be mindful.

Mindfulness is an effortless, simple process that consists of drawing novel distinctions, that is, noticing new things. The more we notice, the more we become aware of how things change depending on the context and perspective from which they are viewed. Mindfulness requires, however, that we give up the fixed ways in which we've learned to look at the world. Most of us confuse the stability of our mind-sets with the stability of the underlying phenomena, and we come to think that things are, will always be, and even need to be a particular way without recognizing how they may also vary. It isn't as though we need or want to be so rigid. We celebrate as creative those who show us how the commonplace may be made different. Many of the mind-sets that hold us back, that deny us our own mindful creativity, are culturally reinforced roadblocks.

Learning how to remove the roadblocks that keep us from a more creative life can bring benefits to the rest of our lives. We may be able to learn to be mindfully creative in all respects and at all times. If we would prosper from this mindfulness, why is the path to creative engagement so often blocked? As much as we'd love to play the recorder or write poetry, it's easier and safer to put it off because we are afraid of making fools of ourselves. Of course, we know we shouldn't worry about what other people think, but we do. Or when we actually give writing or drawing a try, the trying turns out to be more terrifying still, and we too quickly put our creative activity aside. Something interferes with just enjoying painting or playing an instrument for the pleasure it brings us.

Most of us don't really understand what keeps us from doing things that we are otherwise drawn to. The answers to that question interest me, both as a psychologist and as an artist. What exactly are the obstacles that keep people from engaging in a more creative life? How do these obstacles prevent us from getting started and then from more fully enjoying creative pursuits? Can we learn to engage our creative interests on the terms we seek? What would be the benefits of doing so? I have studied exactly these questions in my scientific life, and I know there are answers that can help virtually anyone become creatively engaged. As an artist, I have seen for myself how a creative endeavor, done mindfully, can teach us to lead more rewarding lives in all respects.

Mindfulness, and its counterpart, mindlessness, are states of mind that I've studied and written about for many years, and I know how potent a force mindfulness can be. As important, I know that people can learn to remake their ways of thinking to be more mindful. In my experience, each of us has the potential for a renaissance, an age defined by a creative, purposeful, and engaged life. It doesn't matter whether the creative work we choose is painting, dance, fiction, poetry, or music. What matters is pursuing it mindfully. How do we get from beginning some new activity to a personal renaissance? Learning what things stand in the way of our comfortably engaging in some leisure activity, and how to break down these roadblocks as we experience them provides the practice we need to deal with our more familiar stresses and fears. Once examined through this new lens, many of our "problems" fall by the roadside. We can, it turns out, *pursue art for art's sake and art for life's sake*, and it matters little what that art is. Any creative activity can have a powerful effect on our lives if we pursue it mindfully and recognize the ways in which old familiar fears and habits can be set aside to make room for the personal renaissance we seek.

I also know from personal experience and scientific study that people can, through the pursuit of their creative interests, enjoy the many benefits of a mindful life. We need not be trapped by fixed mind-sets, we can learn to recategorize the world, to change the way in which we define and approach events and our impressions of them. We can gain an enhanced receptivity to new information and an openness to new points of view. A mindful life can also give us increased control over the context of our lives and a new appreciation of process over outcome.

It doesn't matter what we choose to do. For my personal renaissance I chose painting. Rather than study any particular school of art, such as Abstract Expressionism or Pop Art, or even define myself as self-taught (which itself turns out to be another school), I wanted to begin a new group or school: *Un-*

taught Art. It is a school unlike any other you may be familiar with. The defining characteristic of Untaught Art is the pursuit of creativity with attention to the process of engagement, rather than a search for the rules that define it. The nature of being schooled is that once we learn how to do something, too often we stop experimenting, learning, and having fun. We proceed mindlessly. The alternative I'm proposing will soon become evident. Entering into something new, without rules to go by, doesn't come to us easily. We have been taught to believe that rules will make it easier for us to find our way. In fact, rules often blind us to what we most want to enjoy in creative activity. Most important, worrying too much about learning the rules usually keeps us from ever engaging in that activity in the first place. We worry that we won't have the talent to learn the rules; we worry that we should already know the rules; and we especially worry that if we don't know the rules, others will dismiss us. The truth is, we're often better off not knowing the rules. When we know them, we run the great risk of mindlessly following them, obviating the potential enjoyment and personal growth the activity could otherwise provide. In general, when we're rule-bound, we mindlessly focus on details and often end up missing the whole. On some occasions we're so focused on the whole that we're blind to the details. Both whole and part are worthy of our mindfulness.

A woman once visited Henri Matisse in his studio and, after examining a painting he had just finished, declared to him, "The arm of this woman is much too long." His reply was quick. "But, madame, you are mistaken. This is not a woman, this is a painting." How many of us, like that woman, have mindlessly applied the rules only to miss the masterpiece before us? No matter how hard we might try to make it otherwise, if we *do* take the chance and, say, "paint," our painting will only be a painting. We will never be able to create a three-dimensional, breathing person on a canvas, so why not paint what we like: two heads, extra long legs, no eyes, whatever we wish? It's time to learn to do it our own way.

The Essence of Mindfulness

Nothing is a waste of time if you use the experience wisely.
AUGUSTE RODIN

Before the airport in Provincetown, Massachusetts, was renovated, a large glass wall faced out over the runway. A few years ago, while waiting for a friend to arrive, I asked the person behind the counter when the flight from Boston was expected. She replied that it was on time and should arrive soon. A short while later a plane taxied up to the terminal in full view. I was standing less than two feet from the ticket agent, and there was no one else in the small airport, just the two of us. Was this my friend's flight? Rather than simply lean over and confirm that the plane right in front of us was the flight I was awaiting, she ritually picked up a microphone and announced the flight's arrival over the public address system.

We've all experienced mindlessness in our lives, those instances when someone's actions (often our own) are characterized by an entrapment in old categories, automatic behavior, and a lack of awareness of the world at hand. Early in my academic career, I frequently found myself frustrated by the mindless behavior I saw around me. People did not seem to be acting in a way that I thought was sensible. When I moved from New York City to Cambridge, I began to notice things like the lines at the bank. In one line there would be two people, and in others there would be five or more. Why didn't anyone join the shorter line? Why were smart people not making use of the detailed information available to them? Was I at times acting this way as well? Indeed I was. What I realized, though, was that in a different context our old behavior made sense.

I decided to conduct experiments to assess how mindlessness comes about and how pervasive it might be, and I have been studying it ever since. An important discovery I made was that we teach ourselves to be mindless in two very different ways: through repetition and through a single exposure to a piece of information. The first way is quite familiar. Most of us have had the experience, for example, of getting in the car to drive someplace familiar, like the office, then realizing, as if all of a sudden, that we have arrived. We made a large part of our trip on "automatic pilot," as we sometimes call mindless behavior. Sometimes we quite deliberately cultivate mindlessness in this way, as when we learn a skill by practicing until it becomes "second nature" to us. It seems sensible to do so. We want to learn the new skill so well that we don't have to think about it. The problem is that, if we are too successful, it might not occur to us to question the way we are doings things in situations outside the context in which we've learned it, even when it would be to our advantage to do so.

The second way in which we become mindless is particularly important: when we hear or read something and accept it without question. Most of what we know about the world or ourselves we have mindlessly learned in exactly this way. In *The Power of Mindful Learning,* I wrote about one example of my own mindlessness that I'm particularly fond of. I was at a friend's house for dinner and noticed that the table was set with the fork on the right side of the plate. I felt as though some natural law had been violated. The fork "goes" on the left side! Anything else just felt wrong. I felt this way in spite of the fact that

I could imagine many reasons why it might be better for the fork to be placed on the right.

I thought about how I had learned this rule. I had never learned a rationale for the best way to set a table. Rather, when I was a child, my mother simply told me that the fork goes on the left. From that day forth I have been destined to put it there, no matter what circumstances might suggest doing otherwise. But was this the best place for a fork? Why do I care where the fork is placed anyway? I had become trapped, unaware that what I had learned about setting tables was locked in place forever.[1]

So, what does setting tables have to do with creativity? It is in exactly this way that we have accepted the roadblocks that stand in the way of our mindful creativity—when we mindlessly follow rules we have learned about ourselves and the world. What's more, like a driver headed to work every morning, we use them repeatedly without any rethinking. Whether we become mindless over time or on initial exposure to information, we unwittingly lock ourselves into a single understanding of that information.

In many small ways we have learned to become mindless without questioning why we do so. At some point early in my life, to take another example, I learned that horses are herbivores, that they don't eat meat. Recently, I was at an equestrian event and a friend asked me to watch his horse while he went to get him a hot dog. I said that I would be happy to do so, but I added that he should instead look for an apple, since horses don't eat meat. What little I had learned about the eating habits of horses I had learned as an absolute, without any context, and I never thought to question whether it might not always be true. This is, of course, the way in which we learn most facts, and it is why we are frequently in error but rarely in doubt. Anyway, my friend soon reappeared with a hot dog and of course the horse promptly ate it. It may be generally true that horses don't eat meat, but someone forgot to tell my friend's horse.

So who cares if horses like hot dogs? Not many of us, but often our mindless acceptance of rules has very important consequences. Those of us who learned to drive many years ago were taught that if we needed to stop the car on a slippery surface, the safest way was to slowly, gently pump the brake. But most new cars have antilock brakes. Now, when stopping on a slippery surface, the safest thing to do is step on the brake firmly and hold it down. Most of us, however, will still gently pump the brakes during a skid. What was once safe is now dangerous. The context has changed, but our behavior remains the same.

How is it that we don't recognize that we've slipped into a particular mind-set, that we're mindlessly accepting and holding on to information? We don't notice precisely because we are "not there" to notice—to notice, we would need to be mindful. The question is more than academic. My research has revealed that our mindlessness can be very costly and that an increase in mindfulness results in an increase in competence, health and longevity, happiness, creativity, charisma, and makes us more satisfied with our work, to name a few of the findings.

The Value of Uncertainty

My favorite thing is to go where I've never been.
DIANE ARBUS

Where we are is where we've never been.
ELLEN J. LANGER

We don't often question information when it comes to us from an authority or is presented in absolute and unconditional language. We simply accept it and become trapped in a fixed mind-set, oblivious to the fact that authorities are sometimes wrong or overstate their case, or that language can be highly manipulative. Indeed, most all the information passed on to us is couched in such absolute language. A child is told that a family consists of "a mommy, a daddy, and a child," and all is fine until one parent leaves home. Then, just like when the fork is placed to the right of the plate, the child doesn't feel right when now told, "We are still a family." It would be much better if the child were taught that one understanding of a family is a mother, a father, and a child, but there are others. Then there wouldn't be such a problem were the circumstances to change.

The language of authority too often binds us to a single perspective, one that limits our ability to respond creatively to the world. There is, however, a better way available, one that allows for a more mindful use of information. As students of general semantics say, the map is not the territory. By presenting (and accepting) information conditionally, we can enhance its usefulness across many contexts.[2]

In order to investigate how language can limit or enhance our ability to use information, psychologist Alison Piper and I conducted a study in which we used either absolute or conditional language. We showed one group of participants unfamiliar objects using absolute language and another group the same objects using conditional language. For example, the first group was told that one of the objects "was" a dog's chew toy, the second that it "could be" a dog's chew toy. Conditional language implicitly suggested to the second group that the objects under certain conditions might not be just what we chose to call them. After we had presented all the objects, we gave both groups a form, and asked them to evaluate the objects from most to least expensive. After they had begun to write, we told them that we didn't have any more forms and we had made an error in our instructions. It was supposed to be from least to most expensive. Who would think to use the "chew toy" as an eraser? The answer was that only those in the second group, who were told the object "could be" a dog's chew toy, did so. The names we give to things often denote only one way they can be understood. If we learn their names as if "the map is the territory," then creative, mindful uses of the objects will not occur to us.

I'm often told that there must be some value in our mindlessness, especially when I'm asked whether automatic behavior doesn't make life faster and easier for people. Not having to think about things is more efficient, or so the argument goes. This line of thought deserves special attention, starting with asking, How often is speed really of the essence? We may achieve the same response either mindfully or mindlessly, but as we will see, when we choose to respond mindfully, the difference in speed is likely to be trivial, but the other consequences of mindfully or mindlessly responding are not. People correctly assume that we cannot be in a constant state of mindfully drawing distinctions about everything. It would seem, then, that the alternative is to be mindless with respect to some things so we can be mindful of others.

We need another alternative. Mindlessness freezes our responses and closes us off to the possibility of change. To argue that mindlessness is rarely, if ever, beneficial is really to argue that we do not want to close ourselves off to possibility. Another alternative is to be either mindful with respect to some particular content or "potentially" mindful. We don't want to learn about anything in such a way that we take as a given that now we know it for certain. Things change. We may not want to notice the myriad ways each cornflake is different from the others, for example, but we also do not want to be so automatic in what we do notice that we fail to see if a metal nut has slipped into the bowl. Eating a mindful breakfast can take the same time as eating a mindless breakfast, not to mention be more pleasurable and safer.

In situations where milliseconds might matter, as when a driver must swerve to avoid hitting a child, it is also arguable that if we were mindfully driving in the first place, we would not have found ourselves needing to avoid disaster in the second place. When mindful, we often avert the danger not yet arisen. Regardless, milliseconds are unlikely to be of the essence in our search for engagement with a more creative life, so I need not pursue the issue any more in this context.[3]

Appreciating uncertainty, however, *is* relevant. We don't realize the power of uncertainty. Most aspects of our culture currently lead us to try to reduce or eliminate uncertainty, which is the essence of mindlessness. We learn to do so in order to know what things are, so that we can control them. Instead, we should consider exploiting the power of uncertainty, so that we can learn what things can become and so that we can become more than we previously thought possible.

The antidote, then, is to avoid becoming mindless and to learn to be more mindful, which we can do by understanding the differences between the two states of mind. Mindfulness makes us sensitive to context and perspective. When we are mindless, our behavior is governed by rules and routines. Essentially we freeze our understanding and become oblivious to subtle changes that would have led us to act differently if only we were aware of them. In contrast, when we are mindful, our behavior may be guided (not governed) by rules and routines, but we stay sensitive to the ways our situation changes. When we are mindless, we are trapped in rigid mind-sets, oblivious to context or perspective. When we are mindful, we are actively drawing novel distinctions rather than relying on distinctions drawn in the past.

And it is just these rules, routines, and mind-sets that are the roadblocks to living a more creative life. People often recognize that the concepts of mindfulness as I describe them are similar to those found in Eastern religions. But mindfulness as I've researched it comes about in a different, more immediate way. My work on mindfulness springs from a Western, scientific perspective. For me, the two ways of becoming mindful are not at odds with each other. Becoming more mindful does not involve achieving some altered state of consciousness through years of meditation. It requires, rather, learning to switch modes of thinking about ourselves and the world. It is very easy to learn to be mindful, which makes doing so appealing to those unwilling to sit still for twenty minutes twice a day. Mindfulness is simply the process of noticing new things. It is seeing the similarities in things thought different and the differences in things taken to be similar.

A Personal Renaissance

Every child is an artist. The problem is how to remain an artist once he grows up.
PABLO PICASSO

A personal renaissance is, in its essence, an awakening. It's only after we've been awakened that we realize how much of our lives we've actually slept through. My days are exciting. I smile so often that people are always asking me what I'm smiling about, as if some unusual event has just occurred. In the past I didn't know, and on occasion the search for an answer took the smile away. Yesterday was different.

It started with an idea. I picked up an old window upon which I had painted either a person or a dog in each of the six small panes. I had wanted to do more with it, and I thought to put a photograph of my paintings, each of different rooms in a house, behind each piece of glass, providing a background for each of the figures. I went through files of my paintings on my computer, selected the photos I liked, reduced them a bit, and printed them out. Rather than measure anything, I flew by the seat of my pants—my favorite way to travel—and I had to make several copies of some of the paintings to get the size right.

The process didn't go smoothly. The window was old and its paint chipped. Every time I tried to fit the paper with the photo against the glass pane, more of the paint came off, leaving unattractive paint chips on the glass. I'd take the photo out, clean the glass, reinstall the photo, and it would happen again. Finally, I was able to clean the glass and see a relatively unobstructed view of the photo. But rather than being frustrated, I was totally consumed by the activity until it was time to leave for work. I went to my office feeling elated, met with my students to design two new experiments, and taught my seminar. When I returned home, I again looked at my creation and thought it was interesting, but I decided that it didn't quite make it—whatever that means.

Here is where my personal renaissance offered an important difference to me, changing the way I felt about the experience. I didn't feel dejected at my failed attempt: I was too aware of the enlivening aspect of simply having created the piece. I'm still excited when I think about changing the paintings in the window. I don't know if it will work, but that is part of the fun. In fact, if I knew for certain that a new idea would work, constructing it would probably seem tedious instead of exciting. There wouldn't be any choices for me to make, and no reason to "be there" as the outcome unfolds. I'm not worried about what anyone else will think of it, about making mistakes, or about how someone else might do it better, I'm just going to do it. This is the way I do most things, and my ability to just do it and enjoy the doing is the reason people often ask me why I'm smiling.

The Balinese don't have a word for art, they don't need one. Everything they do they try to become totally engaged in, everything is raised to the level of art. This is not the case for most of us. There are too many roadblocks that prevent us from such total engagement, and they, unnecessarily, are taken as part and parcel of everyday life. They tend to rule our everyday lives.

In fact, a more creative life, like the Balinese enjoy, is available to us if we choose it. For example, most of us cook every day, but instead of creating our meals, we prepare them, treating each as though the meal were a chore. Often we don't consider being creative about it because we need to rush to work. We blindly follow recipes and make meals the way we always made them; cooking is easier that way and presents fewer problems. We put so many potential pleasures aside and ironically complain of boredom. What would be the cost if we decided to take a new approach? Perhaps it would take a bit longer or the results, as in the case of mindfully cooking, might not taste as good as we had hoped. But think about the benefits if we actually made choices instead of following a script. New experiences, new tastes, new foods would all be open to us. The costs of trying, if any, are minimal; the benefits, which are certain, can enliven, engage, and make us mindful once again. But we hold back, ready with too many reasons not to engage in even modest mindfully creative activities. And the cost of that inaction is palpable—we give up our greatest chance at being authentic, of living the life we really want to live.

The Essence of a Personal Renaissance

You can't make an architect. But you can . . . open the doors and windows
toward the light as you see it.
FRANK LLOYD WRIGHT

Make it new.
EZRA POUND

Creativity and mindfulness are natural partners. Understanding how to think mindfully is the best way to break through the roadblocks that keep us from developing our creative selves. Then, once we've begun to exercise it, creative expression can be a valuable way to explore these new modes of mindful thinking.

When we are mindful we feel centered, and of course, this is where we'd prefer to be. But social situations can be so complex that we often get thrown off our center and don't realize it. We get caught in a script that dictates how we think we should behave and don't realize that we don't need to follow the script until much later, if we realize it at all. We get pulled in, becoming reactive rather than active. "I said this because he said that." "I did this because you did that." We give up control over our behavior and our emotions. At this point, we are even more likely to play out a mindless script that tells us how we should think, act, and feel. Later, we may say that the other person "pushed our buttons," as if the interaction could not have taken a different turn. Of course, we could have chosen to do otherwise if we were in the present to make the choice.

The more mindful we are, the more choices we have and the less reactive we become. We don't realize when we are mindless. We're not there to notice. If, however, we allowed ourselves to become fully engaged in some new activity, over time we could more easily compare how we feel when we are mindfully engaged with how we feel at other times. The more experience we have with being mindfully creative, the sooner we will recognize when we are simply acting out a script and the sooner we can return to being centered. When we are mindfully engaged, we are essentially writing our own script and are free to choose to make changes at any point. When we are mindfully creative, we are being authentic.

What are the roadblocks that keep us from creative pursuit? They are the same things that throw us off center in the activities in which we engage at home or at work, with family, friends, or strangers. The things that throw us off center are so much a part of what we've accepted as normal that we rarely question them. We believe that there is a "right" way of doing things; that some people do them better than others; that it is human to make mistakes; that most of us don't have talent; that if we pretend we can "get by," and that this would be preferable to trying to engage the task at which we are sure to be unsuccessful anyway. Each of these mind-sets plays into the others. If I fear making mistakes, for example, I won't fully engage myself in the task. Instead I mindlessly follow a script for how to avoid them. If I am following a script, then I am not centered in the present, which could easily result in my making more "mistakes." And so the cycle continues.

Those are not our only choices, and starting a creative activity is an easy way for us to begin a personal renaissance. Once we remove the roadblocks that stand in the way of our creative pursuit, we will come to recognize when we are off center, following a script rather than being authentic. With that recognition, we can decide to be authentic and not cut off. Mindfully engaging a new activity is enlivening and rewarding in its own right. By repeated experience with being centered, in the present, and truer to ourselves, we will be less tolerant of feeling less so. This creates no problem, because the roadblocks to mindful creativity are the same roadblocks that prevent a more mindful life.

Picasso once admitted, "I don't know in advance what I am going to put on canvas any more than I decide beforehand what colors I am going to use." If we know everything in advance, then we will inevitably proceed mindlessly and we will miss the joy of the activity. Instead of trying to make the "right" decision, we might consider just doing "it" and creating it into something that feels right.

In the end, my work on learning to engage ourselves creatively and mindfully is focused on teaching people what I have learned about happiness. For years I would wonder why people didn't just "do it," why they didn't avail themselves of the opportunities around them and the talents they clearly possessed. My work has led me to conclude that the loneliness, boredom, and feelings of inadequacy people experience are usually the results of a lack of connection with themselves.

Unhappiness and self-centeredness go hand in hand. Ironically, a self that is absorbed in itself may be a self that is cut off from itself. When we stop experiencing ourselves, we end up treating ourselves as objects of evaluation. And, inevitably, that is a negative experience. To truly be mindful, it would behoove us to engage or experience something outside of or other than ourselves.

And that is the essence of a personal renaissance, to learn to act and engage with ourselves mindfully, creatively, actively, and happily.

2

Becoming Authentic

I am an artist . . . I am here to live out loud.
ÉMILE ZOLA

Ironically say I, the feeling of egolessness, is the journey home and the experience of the mindful self.
VIRGINIA WOOLF

WHAT DO WE MEAN WHEN WE ATTRIBUTE SOMETHING TO BEGINner's luck, and why do some people seem to have beginner's luck and not others? Is it luck or is there something else at work? If the phenomenon were reliable, that is, if some people really do have it, it could not really be luck. The very nature of luck or chance is that it is random. Two possible explanations come to mind. The first and less interesting one is that there is really no such thing as beginner's luck. Sometimes beginners are successful, and just as often or as unpredictably they are not. When they are, we explain it as beginner's luck.

The second explanation takes as its starting point that there is such a thing as beginner's luck, but it supposes that the results are anything but random. When we are worried about appearing incompetent, we frequently get in our own way and become stressed and self-conscious. When we begin something new—paint for the first time, try hitting a golf ball, or write our first story—we usually have very low expectations for ourselves, if we have any at all. Without undue concern for our performance as beginners, we plunge in, letting the task, not problematic self-talk, lead us. At the beginning, we may proceed more mindfully than we will later, when we have come to expect too much from ourselves. In this way, beginner's luck may be the result of mindful engagement.

I've experienced it. I had to forgo playing tennis one winter, spring, and most of the summer because of a broken ankle. When I picked up my tennis racket again in August, I was surprised at how well I played. I was not a beginner, but I wasn't playing with all the baggage I had when I got hurt. I was absorbed in the experience of being back on the court, and I played well because I simply hit the ball when it came to me. I didn't get into discussions with myself about how important it was to do so or what I would look like if I hit a bad shot. Perhaps we don't have to be beginners to have beginner's luck. We just need to let ourselves be in the present, and when we do, we tap into our authentic self—our natural, mindfully creative self.

In a wonderful book on the art of personal narrative, *The Situation and the Story,* Vivian Gornick convincingly demonstrates what can be achieved when essay writing leads to authenticity. Using passages from William Hazlitt, Virginia Woolf, and James Baldwin, for example, she illustrates that, although these writers may not have any greater knowledge about themselves than anyone else, "they know who they are at the moment of writing." When Joan Didion explores her frequent migraines in the essay "In Bed," the experience is so real that we willingly take on the journey with her and learn how our downfalls can be assets, that even migraine headaches are useful. As Gornick explains, we believe Didion because we see how her insights are born at "the moment of the writing." That is, she is mindful. In exploring her migraines, she discovers that her initial response was only one way to experience them. The reader can feel the honesty as Didion writes so closely from her self, from an undisguised self. This is true of all the writers in Gornick's book.

There is no pretense, no public to impress. It is as though we are inside their heads watching them grow. They search for the "inviolable self," a self that is available to all of us. If we pick up a pen or sit down at the computer to explore something we care about and do so honestly, we will not know at the outset where we are going to end up. We do know, however, that the process will be enlivening.[1]

My claim is that anyone can be mindfully creative. I'm not saying, "I have no talent so if I can do it anyone can," which may or may not be true. I am saying that now that I have a pretty good idea of what it takes to be creative, I can state with confidence that virtually anyone can be. When we break down any task to smaller parts, much of the mystery and the concomitant fear of trying disappear. To make a living at being a professional artist (or writer, musician, et cetera) is a matter for someone else to explore. My interest here is in our taking up a creative endeavor as a means of getting closer to who we can be, the matter of becoming authentic. It's really about the journey home.

The fact is that most of us pretend we live our lives fully engaged because we think we can get away with it. But by pretending, we rob ourselves of the authenticity that comes from mindful engagement. This is a heavy price to pay, especially because, as we will soon see, people aren't really being fooled anyway. We come to believe that things are good or bad, that some can but others can't and our mistakes reveal we're in the "can't" group, and that we have no talent, so why should we even try?

Mindfulness Is Visible

It is not the language of painters but the language of nature which one should listen to, the feeling for the things themselves, for reality, is more important than the feeling for pictures.
VINCENT VAN GOGH

How often have we heard that someone "has a real presence" or that "the room seems to light up when she walks in"? We all know such people, but few of us can easily point to why it is that they seem special. I've conducted research which has shown that when people are coached to be more mindful in a situation, those around them are likely to see them as more charismatic and more genuine.[2] If mindful creativity can help us become more authentic and enhance the way people think of us, to what extent are the costs of denying ourselves the pleasures of mindfulness also apparent?

Most people at some time or another have hidden their true feelings from others or "put up a good front" in order to hide something. Usually doing so means that we follow whatever script we think is relevant for the particular moment and audience. We behave the way we think we should behave, or the way we think others think we should behave, shutting down our ongoing feelings or understanding about the world. Adults do this all the time to children, in the belief that they should be protected from the adult world and adult feelings. Often I've heard of parents who hide the difficulties in their relationship for "the sake of the children." Whenever we work from scripts and not from our experience, we are mindlessly approaching the situation, taking our cues from fixed beliefs about what is right, oblivious to alternatives and ignoring the variation of the situation.

I have often wondered whether hiding our authentic selves in this way really works, and whether others, especially children, aren't more sensitive to our true states of mind than we realize. Those questions led me to explore more deeply whether our mindfulness is visible to others. I decided, though, that I wouldn't start with children; I would start with animals.

I have long noticed that my dogs seem sensitive to my thoughts. To be sure, most dog owners have probably noticed that their dogs run out of the room or hide under the furniture when tempers get out of control. My observations even suggested to me that dogs could be used as barometers of our mindfulness. Obviously we don't need our dogs' perception much once the screaming begins, but it might prove useful during times of subtle stress. If the dogs pick it up, the children probably do. But I am getting ahead of myself.

Determined to test the theory, I brought my two dogs to my lab. I asked two students to call one of the dogs by name, with one student doing so while in a mindful state and one mindlessly reciting an overlearned nursery rhyme to herself. The dog went to the mindful student. We repeated this several times, varying which student was mindful and on which side the mindful student stood. The dog did not always race to the mindful person, but he did show a preference. It may be the effect was small or perhaps my students, steeped in how to be mindful, were not easily able to be mindless.

Wanting to explore the idea more, I went to a local kennel and tried again. We'd take a dog into a small room. One of the staff members mindlessly repeated a nursery rhyme to herself and another staff person mindfully told herself how this dog was different from others of its breed. The question was, To whom would the dog go, the mindful or the mindless person?

I stood behind a door with a window and timed how quickly the dog approached the staff member it chose. I was unaware of which staff member was mindful and which mindless. It seemed at first a relatively straightforward experiment, but it wasn't. The dogs in the adjoining room made a racket that could be heard in both rooms. Their barking may not have been the reason, but the dogs in the study often wouldn't cooperate. And when they did, they showed a preference for the person who fed them that overrode my attempts to manipulate a mindful state. When we removed this confound (by using staff who didn't feed them), there was some evidence that the dogs recognized and preferred the mindful person, but the effect wasn't strong enough to draw any firm conclusions.

We next tried the experiment using only one staff person, who was mindful or mindless without my knowing which. This seemed to work better. But there was another problem: the staff came to the experiment with the notion that a dog would approach them more quickly when they were paying more attention to the dog, so their eye contact increased when they were being mindful, which made the data hard to decipher.

I was loathe to give up the idea that dogs can sense when we are mindful, however, so we made one more attempt. We gave a questionnaire to dog owners that asked them to try certain exercises with their dogs and tell us their results. Unbeknownst to them, the exercises suggested specific thoughts to place them in a mindful or a mindless state. We asked the subjects to have their dogs sit about four feet in front of them and then asked them to think their assigned thought for a period of time. Afterward, we asked them to answer some questions about their dogs' behaviors. For the first time in my research career, out of over one hundred questionnaires distributed, not one person returned a completed form. In following up with some of the people who had not responded, I learned that the dogs would not sit still long enough for the owners to answer our questions.

It was becoming clear that this experiment was not going to provide the answer to whether dogs could detect our subtle cues any time soon. To run the study properly became more of an ordeal than my student collaborators were eager to spend their time on. Still interested and undeterred, I left dogs behind to join the sea lions and dolphins. Several of my students, Sarit Golub, Matt Cohen, and David Borden, were involved in this program of research. It began at the New England Aquarium, where we examined the interaction of sea lions and their trainers. The staff was extremely helpful, and those in charge held to the belief that sea lions have people preferences. In fact, several believed that the sea lions knew them better than most people did. The question was, Were these preferences a function of the trainers' mindfulness? To assess this, we first administered the Langer Mindfulness Scale to twelve trainers.

Over the next several months, the head trainer (who was unaware of the other trainers' mindfulness scores) systematically observed the sea lions' interaction with their trainers, noting in particular the approach behavior of the sea lions. The more mindful the trainer, the more the sea lions showed these approach behaviors.

The sea lions preferred the trainers who scored better on the mindfulness scale. One could consider several hypotheses as to why the sea lions have this preference. It may be that when they are being fed by humans, the humans are more mindful. One might expect this to be the case, because the trainers enjoy the attention they get from the sea lions at feeding time. Also, when food is at stake, the sea lions tend to become more aggressive, so the trainers need to be on their toes. An alternative hypothesis is that mindfulness itself is rewarding to a sea lion.

The point of our investigation was to see whether sea lions were aware of our mindfulness, whatever the reason for the awareness. To be more certain of this relationship, it was important to do a more formal experiment. We did this with the generous help of the director of the Dolphin Adventure in Puerto Vallarta, Mexico. I was interested to learn that the trainers there also felt the dolphins prefer to swim with some tourists more than others. I wondered whether the dolphins were preferring some people because they are more mindful. Thirty-nine trainers and seven dolphins enabled us to test our hypothesis.

It is well known that dolphins are intelligent animals. The director of the center told us the dolphins are rewarded with their favorite fish in exchange for retrieving the bits of paper that find their way into the pools. One dolphin, they discovered, learned to tear any paper he found into several pieces, increasing the reward. Soon thereafter, another dolphin started doing the same. They are clearly intelligent, but could they discern mindfulness in people?

Our approach was a little different this time. I had the trainers give the Langer Mindfulness Scale to willing tourists who were about to swim with the dolphins. After they did so, the trainers noted with which swimmers the dolphins spent the most time. Although the dolphins are trained to spend time with each tourist, they still spend more time with some tourists than with others. And we found there was a correlation: the dolphins spent the least time with those swimmers whose mindfulness scores were the lowest. We hypothesized that the preference that dolphins have regarding people is at least in part a function of the tourists' states of mindfulness. But it was not entirely clear if the dolphins in our study were responding to the mindfulness of the tourists or to something else mindful people may have in common.

To get closer to answering our questions, we ran a controlled experiment in which trainers were instructed in what kind of thoughts to have—mindful or mindless. Then we timed the dolphins' approach to them and how long the dolphins stayed. It appears that animals such as those we tested are in some way aware of human mindfulness. They swam faster and stayed longer when the trainer was mindful. It could be some subtle nonverbal cue that occurs when we are mindful, a change in scent we give off with changes in consciousness, or some other yet-to-be-determined factor.

We've asked whether dogs could be emotional barometers to waken people to the possibility that pretending "for the child's sake" may be misguided. The child's awareness was our major interest at the time, so it seemed best to leave the animal kingdom, as much fun as it provided us, and return to a direct test of our hypothesis.

When we are mindful, do others know? Many popular expressions like "The light's on but nobody's home" or "He has only one oar in the water" tell us people seem to know when others are mindless. We often feel we can tell when someone is pretending to think or feel a certain way. When people are pretending they are following a script written in the past, and scripted behavior is, typically, mindless behavior. A script may have been well conceived, but it usually will not be completely successful because it is being enacted regardless of its current appropriateness. In a very real way, a mindless script is pretense and disingenuousness. If we are instead situated in the present, taking our cues from the current context, we are more likely to be authentic, and to be perceived as such.

What is the effect of adult mindless pretense on children? If one's mindfulness was not in some way visible, the answer might be, None. We believed otherwise. Matt Cohen, a member of my lab, ran a summer camp for underprivileged youth. We designed an experiment that he conducted at the camp. Adults who interacted with the children were instructed to say nice things during the interaction and to try to make the children like them. When mindful, the adults were instructed to be positive but genuine and to find a way to make the interaction interesting to themselves. They were told to notice how the children changed during the interview. For example, they were asked to notice subtle modulations in voice inflection, posture, and so on. The mindless instructors were asked to pretend they were interested in what the children had to say. After a four-minute interaction, children were given a test of self-esteem. The results were clear: Interacting with a mindless adult pretending to be positive led to a drop in the children's self-esteem. They felt less competent, were less willing to help other campers, and had some negative feelings toward the adult when the adult was mindless.

The Costs of Pretending

The artist need not know very much; best of all let him work instinctively and paint as naturally as he breathes or walks.
EMIL NOLDE

It is not just animals and children who can pick up our mindfulness. John Sviokla and I conducted research a number of years ago in which we asked people to sell magazines to adults mindfully or mindlessly.[3] Subjects were given a sales pitch to memorize so that they could recite it without thinking about it. We divided the subjects into two groups and gave them different instructions on how to approach customers. One group was asked to repeat their pitch exactly the same way with each new customer. The second group was given a more mindful approach. We told them to make each sales pitch new in subtle ways in which only they would know how it differed each time they tried to make a sale. When we later interviewed the customers, they reported that they found the mindful salespeople significantly more charismatic. We have all had experiences of this sort. Consider how annoying salesmen are when they stick to their scripts no matter what you say to them. Or the last time you watched a chorus line, and your eyes were riveted on someone off to the side. His position onstage says that he is less skilled than the lead dancers at the center, but in some way we find him more interesting. If it isn't the size of the part, or any lack of skill in the other dancers, what draws us to him?

It is not just salespeople or members of a chorus line for whom this is relevant. Lab members Christine Kawakami, Judith White, and I explored how authenticity can make its presence felt in the realm of leadership.[4] Although there are many more women in business today than even twenty years ago, women still are not entering the highest leadership positions as often as men.[5] The problem is that the traits that are stereotypically female are not traits associated with leadership. Women are soft, men are effective, or so the stereotype says. Women make more use of nonverbal behaviors that are seen as warm and expressive—leaning forward, making eye contact, and smiling, for instance—than do men. People perceive more masculine stereotypes—cold, competitive, and authoritarian—however, as indicative of greater leadership ability.

Although studies show that both men and women can be effective leaders, most managerial positions are seen as masculine in nature and requiring masculine attributes. Research has shown, however, that women are judged less effective when they behave in ways that aren't considered feminine. Many have made the point that women in business face a difficult choice. If they act "like women," they will be liked but not respected. If they adopt a stereotypic male leadership style, they will be more successful but disliked for stepping outside their traditional gender role. They face a double bind. We tested these assumptions by exploring whether *how* a woman adopts a stereotypically masculine trait determines perceptions of her leadership ability.

We made video clips of women delivering the same persuasive speech. Each of them had memorized a Rotary Club president's speech concerning the group's recent performance. Half of the women were given instructions to be nonverbally cool and half to be warm. Thus, we elicited "male" versus "female" traits. Each woman was videotaped each time she practiced giving the speech. She was instructed to tell us when she felt completely comfortable with it and could deliver it without having to think about the content. We used the tape of the speech right before that overlearned one as a more mindful performance and the one immediately after it as the more mindless performance. We then played the clips for male business leaders and asked them to rate the speakers on their leadership ability.

We found that women who adopted a male leadership style but who were mindful were perceived as more genuine, were better liked, and were perceived to be more effective leaders than those who were less mindful. That is, if mindful, women can behave in a comfortable, warm way and still be seen as effective, because mindfulness is visible and attractive.

It is interesting that, in situations that make us nervous, we turn to stereotyped behavior for fear of being disapproved of, yet mindlessly following a script, as we shall see, causes the very problem we seek to prevent. Not only can people notice if we are "not there" but if we are mindless and thus not there, all that is left of us is our stereotype. When we interact with people mindlessly, we often rely on our stereotypes of them. If we were mindful, by contrast, we would have individuating information about the people.

In research Jesse Preston and I conducted on stereotypes, we took advantage of a stereotype, forgetfulness, that many people have about "old women."[6] People were shown a video clip of one of several older women who were instructed to be mindful or mindless. First, we found that mindful people were liked more, but even more interesting, we found that when these people were mindless, they were more likely to be described in stereotypic terms. For example, when the older woman on the videotape had been instructed to be mindless, she was seen as forgetful and timid. When the women were mindful, they were not seen in these stereotypic ways.

What we know thus far is that when we are mindful we are seen as charismatic, authentic, and more as individuals. We give these positive perceptions up when we are mindless. Similarly, when we follow a script and pretend, even if we are only pretending seemingly harmless things, we essentially rob ourselves. When we feel we'll come up short, we may pretend to be other than we are. If we fail at the pretense, we don't feel good. Failure never or rarely does. But what happens if we succeed? Our research suggests that if we successfully fool others into thinking we are who we think we are not, we rob ourselves of the positive effects of praise. We pretend when we think we should be other than who we are. That's bad enough. Once people praise us for who they think we are but we "know" we are not, we ironically take that as disapproval for who we really are.[7]

Mindful Music

Music is your own experience, your own thoughts, your wisdom. If you don't live it, it won't come out of your horn. They teach you there's a boundary line to music. But, man, there's no boundary line to art.
Charlie Parker

No matter what we are doing, we can do it either mindfully or mindlessly. This is true whether we are with our pets, our children, eating lunch, engaging in conversation, or working. But does mindfulness have an effect on our creative lives? Let's look more closely at this question with regard to music and art, with an understanding that our observations speak to any endeavor in which we may engage.

Musicians know well that playing the same piece over and over can become tedious. I have been told that even those in symphony orchestras can become quite bored playing the same pieces over and over and over again. If they played the piece mindfully, would that eliminate the boredom? And if so, could audiences hear the difference? Composer and conductor Timothy Russell and lab member Noah Eisenkraft joined me in research to investigate whether a more mindful approach to playing would improve both the musicians' and the listeners' experience.[8] We asked the Arizona State Symphony Orchestra to play the finale from Brahms's Symphony No. 1, a very familiar piece to them. We first asked them to play the piece while trying to re-create their best performance of it. We then had them play it again, this time asking them to find subtle ways to make the music new for them. We believed that the first instruction would provoke a more mindless approach to the music, as they tried to replicate a previous, favorite performance, while the second was expected to engage them and result in mindful music making.

Later, we gave all the musicians a questionnaire that asked how much they enjoyed playing the piece and how they tried to make the second performance new. We then played tapes of both performances for approximately 150 members of the orchestra's chorus, some of whom were very knowledgeable about music, and asked them how much they enjoyed each. The musicians overwhelmingly reported that they enjoyed the mindful performance more than the mindless one, some stating that they found the mindful experience enlivening. Almost 90 percent of the audience reported that they heard a clear difference in the two approaches, and more than 80 percent of those who noted a difference preferred the more mindful approach. We repeated a version of this experiment with several orchestras, some given instructions that led them to be mindful and some instructions that led them to be mindless. The findings were the same.

What is true for the professional musician is also true for novice musicians. In research I wrote about in *The Power of Mindful Learning,* our lab conducted a study in which one group of participants learned piano exercises mindfully, that is, without using rote memory techniques. They were asked to change their style of play every few minutes. A control group was asked to practice the exercises in the more traditional way, memorization through repetition, so that playing the exercises becomes like "second nature," that is, mindless. Performances were taperecorded and played for judges who were not aware of the group from which each piece came. The judges rated the mindful performances as more competent and creative than those performed by the mindless group.

Authentic Art

Every artist dips his brush in his own soul,
and paints his own nature into his pictures.
HENRY WARD BEECHER

I have come to believe that, above all else, to be a true artist is to be mindful. Even if someone has all the skills in place, a mindlessly executed work of art is in some sense dead. If that is the case, then no matter what our level of skill, if the art is mindfully engaged, the end result should lead to a positive outcome. That doesn't mean we will all be famous artists, but it does mean that any of us can engage in art successfully.

As I described, I decided to take up painting without trying to learn or follow the rules. I couldn't do otherwise, since I didn't know any of the rules. I decided just to put my heart into it and take the plunge. The first time I tried I had only a wooden shingle and some paint. I wasn't self-conscious about what I was doing because I was just experimenting, passing a rainy day in a new way. I forgot to be afraid, and I got lost in the activity, finding it to be overwhelmingly fun. I painted another piece and then one more, each time observing how enlivened it made me feel, and I realized how important being mindful was to the process. The paintings, to my surprise, had some charm and pleased me. As I described in Chapter 1, one of my first paintings was of a horse that I somehow situated on both sides of a fence at the same time. Even though it wasn't "right," it engaged me as the artist, and it engaged people who saw it. To my mind, it works because it is authentic, it says something about me and the process of creating it. I believe that in authenticity lies the success we can all share in creative engagement.

Soon thereafter, I painted a woman lying on the very edge of a bed with a book in her hand and a dog at her feet. When I had finished, I noticed that the small dressers on each side of the bed were cockeyed, yet they somehow added to the work. For no particular reason, I had painted a similar scene on a small piece of glass. My partner Nancy told me that she loved the painting but wished I had done it on a canvas instead. To surprise her, I found a small canvas and reproduced the painting on it. This time, the dressers were much straighter, but I thought the painting had lost some of its charm. I showed it to Nancy, who still liked it but mentioned that she wished I had painted it on a larger canvas. Ever willing to please, I found a larger canvas and painted a third and final version. I noticed that each time I had enjoyed the activity less. I had invested less of myself in each subsequent painting. Knowing just where I needed to go and going there, rather than discovering some new place along the way, meant that I was painting less mindfully than before. Nancy and I both felt that the final painting was not as good as the more mindfully created original. Somehow, it seemed clear, my diminished interest in the painting was present on the canvas and visible to others.

Was I correct to think so? Allan Filipowicz, Nikko Sommaripa, and I decided to find out.[9] We recruited a group of people to make drawings and then copy their drawings, varying the conditions under which they did so. We had one group draw a dog, then make a copy of it, copy it again, and copy it one last time. One might expect the drawings would get better and better with practice, but we expected that each copy would be produced more mindlessly as our subjects attempted to get through the assigned task. We are not typically taught to do the "same" thing differently, rather we are too often told to repeat things until we don't have to think about them anymore. That is, we are more often taught to learn to do things mindlessly. Moreover, not just by design but by desire, we become wedded to our work and are afraid to change it for fear of making it worse.

We gave a second group similar instructions, except that they were asked to make the last copy new in subtle ways that would not be obvious to anyone other than themselves. We expected that the last, mindful copy would be best. Like Monet's haystacks, they are at once the same but different.

Finally, we varied whether or not the participants were given a choice of what to draw. We believed that drawing without choice would engender mindlessness. To make sure the content was similar so that we could compare the original and the copies created under choice or no choice, we subtly persuaded everyone to draw a dog. The choice group was told that we had enough of the other drawings so we'd really appreciate it if they drew a dog, but the choice was theirs. They all complied. Our prediction was that the mindful drawings would be preferred to those less mindfully created, whether their mindfulness came about by intentionally making it new or through making choices.

Our first attempts are not necessarily the most mindful. I had discussed my own experiences before we began this research with my friend Anthony Russo, a well-known illustrator and artist. He told me he believes that his first drawing is often not as mindful as the second because he feels the first is done out of obligation if he's working on a commission. Initially, he does what is required of him, but once he chooses to free himself, his illustrations get better and better.

We found that people do indeed prefer art that is mindfully created. It is less perfect and more pleasing. This will be a theme we will return to again and again: we seek perfection and get frozen by the thought of our imperfection. This is ironic in that the outcomes we seek are more likely to come to our imperfect selves.

In *Mindfulness* I describe a study by the psychologist Anita Karsten in which participants were instructed to write their names repeatedly until they were mentally and physically exhausted. At the moment they felt they couldn't take it anymore, the researcher said the experiment was finished and if they just signed the subject payment form they could go. Although engaging in the same activity, signing their names, this time they did so without signs of exhaustion—in fact, their signatures on the payment forms were closer to their initial signatures than to the last ones in the experiment. The context had changed, so they approached the task with renewed energy. The important difference between Karsten's study and our experiments with music and drawing is that the participants in our studies changed the context for themselves. By making it new for themselves, they produced results that were visible to others.[10]

When we are not pretending or are not mindless in other ways, the products of our labor will have our own signatures. Our fondness for our own mindfully produced work may even lead us to question who decided on the set of standards that bind us in the first place. Our evaluations determine our behavior. We approach things we think good and avoid things we believe bad. We do things we believe we will do well and avoid activities we think we and others will reject. Who determined the criteria for what is good and what is bad? With respect to art, for example, each school or movement is replaced by another that at first is rejected as "bad." We are tyrannized by evaluations, and perhaps we shouldn't be.

The more mindful we are, the less self-conscious we are. The more we know just what we're going to do before we do it, the more opportunity there is to be self-conscious and to proceed mindlessly. Art can make us more mindful, and being more mindful may increase our ability to do and appreciate art.

Manet spent his life painting works that seem to be full of contradictions and a lack of perspective. Although now considered a master, during his lifetime he was always controversial. In part this was because he used his unique vision. He was true to himself whether he painted beggars, prostitutes, or the bourgeoisie. He was interested in producing "not great art, but sincere art." I would call it Mindful Art.

3

The Tyranny of Evaluation

The Balinese do not have a word for art. A word is not necessary when everything is appreciated in the way we tend to value only the work by master artists. The Balinese say they do everything as well as they can.
PRESTON MCCLANAHAN

LAST YEAR, I TRIED PAINTING A PORTRAIT OF MY FRIEND RHODA and brought it to her house for her to see. She admired it, saying all the appropriate things to make me feel good. Then she showed me a portrait of her that another friend had painted. The two looked nothing alike, and mine was clearly the superior painting—the other painting had gotten her all wrong. Of course, I write this in jest, but only half so. Only half because I didn't see Rhoda the way this other artist did, and at first, that impostor painting *did* feel very wrong to me. The woman in that painting seemed much less dynamic than the Rhoda I knew. We both knew and cared for Rhoda well enough to take the time to paint her, but we clearly had different experiences with her to draw from.

In thinking about it, I realized it was odd of me to imagine that two artists would see the same thing when we look at the same subject. Most of us, after all, would agree that our personal experience informs our vision. We've all had the experience of not seeing something right in front of us because we aren't paying attention or simply because we lack interest in it. For example, when you need a new car and decide to consider buying a convertible, you'll suddenly see all the convertibles on the road, which only yesterday you didn't notice. Whether it is shaping how we see the world, or even what we choose to see, our experience, without doubt, colors our perception.

If our experiences inform our vision and our experiences are unique—my day and yours may have common elements, but surely there are some things you do in the course of a day that I do not and vice versa—then we probably do see the "same" thing differently. We don't often acknowledge it, because the generality of language we use tends to hide the differences in our referents. Both you and I might say "I got out of bed this morning and got ready for work" despite the fact that our particular activities this morning were not remotely the same.

Such generality of language leads us to presume, mistakenly, that there exists some objective reality, and that presumption, in turn, leads us to believe that objective evaluation is reasonable. But if we look very closely, we find that while there may be similarities, there really aren't many common properties that run through your unique experiences and mine. What we choose to call "art," for example, differs historically, by medium, taste, style, and any number of other factors. The defining characteristics of art for Plato, who valued representation, were quite different from Picasso's as he was inventing Cubism.

By believing that my portrait of Rhoda—if I'm feeling confident—is better than someone else's, I fail to engage the other painting. As a result, I rob myself of an opportunity to see Rhoda in a new light, through the eyes of this other person. Instead, I look at the painting, form an evaluation of it based on some personal criteria, and then dismiss it. If I could consider it mindfully, however, I might discover that the artist had captured Rhoda in a way that reveals a shyness I've never noticed in her before.

It has been said that the implicit job of artists is to show us, through art, music, or literature, what we would not otherwise have seen, felt, or realized without their perspective. We do tend to consider the work of well-known artists in this light, largely because we think we ought to, because their reputation convinces us that they have something to tell us. But why do we limit this openness to the perspective of others to well-known artists? Why do we tend to discount or ignore another person's perspective even though it may well have much to teach us? If both portraits of Rhoda captured the same person based on different experiences, why couldn't I see the value of the other artist's experience more easily?

The Mindlessness of Evaluation

It terrified me to have an idea that was solely mine to be no longer a part of my mind, but totally public.
MAYA LIN

The tyranny evaluation holds over us is the most important roadblock we need to overcome to achieve a personal renaissance. The most common reason we hesitate when presented with the opportunity to express ourselves creatively is our fear of other people's negative opinions. Studies show that people form evaluations based on their own needs, but we tend to accept other people's evaluations as though they were objective. It's not easy to try something without knowing the outcome, but mindfulness can teach us that not knowing the outcome is actually preferable and that, regardless, the evaluations of others—both good and bad—are not really objective and needn't shape our choices.[1]

Evaluations work just like rules; they dictate our response. We avoid things that lead to bad evaluations, gravitate to those that lead to good evaluations. But following rules can sometimes lead to mindless behavior that is ultimately bad for us. If I'm driving at sixty-five miles an hour during an ice storm, I may be able to argue that I'm following the rules, but the consequences of my rule following aren't likely to be good. It's obvious, of course, that in this case I've applied the rules without regard to the conditions, without thinking about the context.

In the same way, when we make or accept evaluations, we hold the world still, and that's mindless. We are, in essence, saying we don't need to be here, we've ceded our right to choose to the evaluator. We'll just do what's dictated.

In fact, we've been conditioned to act this way throughout our lives. When we're young we're ruled by evaluation—it keeps children in place—and our behavior is very context-driven. In school, we're quiet. We cross the street only on green. As children, we behave in a way that most people can easily understand given the context we're in. As we get older, however, the rules become less clear, which can make us hesitant and more vulnerable. While the advantage to being older is that we are able to choose the context, we can do so only if we are aware that we have choices. That awareness—mindfulness—is the basis of a personal renaissance. With it our behavior is, oddly enough, more consistent because it's based on internal criteria.

Without that awareness, we assume that evaluations exist independent of ourselves. Each day we think and feel and act as if people, objects, and events were good or bad in themselves. Potholes, tax collectors, and divorce are bad, while caviar, philanthropists, and holidays are good. But quite frequently we mindlessly hold on to value judgments that we have attached to various events, objects, and states of the world, even though the world is not fixed. We find something pleasing or displeasing because we choose to see it in a particular way, not because it is inherently so. We are still able to form new judgments in new contexts, but we are too often oblivious to the possibility of doing so.

In reality, things "out there" rarely are self-evidently good or bad. Most important, when we are not locked in by fixed evaluations, we have far more control than we imagine over our well-being. We have control over our experience of the present. The prevalence of value judgments in our lives reveals nothing about the world but much about our minds. We judge and evaluate in order to do or possess what's "good" or "right." We identify the feeling of having what is good or doing what is right with happiness. We are rarely immediately conscious of the real purpose of our evaluations. Evaluation is something we use to make ourselves happy. As we shall see, however, an evaluative mind-set is self-defeating, it brings us unhappiness instead.

Evaluation is central to the way we make sense of our world; almost all of our thoughts are concerned with whether what we or others are doing or thinking is good or bad. Yet in most cases the way we accept or form evaluations is mindless. We pay lip service to the idea that there are two sides to the proverbial coin; we acknowledge that everything has advantages and disadvantages, yet we tend to treat things as good or bad on the balance. A more mindful approach would entail understanding not only that there are advantages and disadvantages to anything we may consider but that each disadvantage is simultaneously an advantage from a different perspective (and vice versa). With this more mindful approach, virtually every unpleasant aspect of our lives could change, and little would hold us back from a personal renaissance.

If a change in our attitude about evaluation is to happen, the most important understanding we need to gain is *All behavior makes sense from the actor's perspective or the actor wouldn't do it.* With this realization we learn to suspect the negative evaluations of people and their actions. And, in turn, we become easier on ourselves.

Artistic Evaluation

The pleasure of criticizing robs us of the pleasure of being moved by some very fine things.
JEAN DE LA BRUYÈRE

The mindless nature of most evaluations imposes a harsh tyranny on all of us, one I've dealt with firsthand as an artist. One of my first paintings was of a horse gleefully kicking his back heels together. I liked the picture a lot—it was great fun, and many people responded to it with encouragement. One friend of mine, however, quickly looked at the painting and informed me that a horse couldn't kick up his heels that way. I was stunned that he would think this was important. I told him that while I was new to painting, I wasn't new to horses. I had painted the horse that way quite intentionally, trying to capture the spirit of the moment rather than the particulars of equine biomechanics. Because he knew I was an inexperienced painter, it was easy for him to suppose that I hadn't meant to paint what I had, and in evaluating the painting in the fixed context of the correct way to draw a horse, he had assumed that I had made a mistake.

It is usually when we are young that we learn to think we are not talented; we are told so by teachers, parents, and other adults. Inevitably, their evaluations are firmly tied to contexts—to particular schools of thought in particular periods of time—although they are typically unaware of it. We accept their evaluations because we are inexperienced: we don't realize that the contexts in which we are being judged really say little about our talent.

There is very little art that is appreciated by everyone, and there is much art that has been critically acclaimed which many people do not like. Some people admire Klee, Pollock, or Kandinsky, and some knowledgeable people do not. Some like Rockwell, Benton, or Balthus, and others do not. It is rare for someone to like all of these artists, but the prices their paintings command attest to the value they have for some people. What's more, values and contexts shift. We all know that van Gogh had no idea that one day he would be one of the most famous and admired artists in the world. Given the disparity in aesthetic tastes, it is peculiar that a single art teacher can determine for us whether we have any artistic talent or not without even questioning the context of her evaluation. Whole realms of experience are denied us because of such individual judgments.

Why is this so? When I look back, I wonder what mark I would have made on a piece of paper that would have led an adult to know that I couldn't eventually paint like Pollock, Mondrian, Miró, or Matisse, given that almost any mark could recall an element of one of their styles. We commonly look to behavior to understand people, even though behavior can be a misleading indicator of the mind responsible for it, and the mindless evaluation of behavior can lead us to judge very sensible people as anything but sensible.

As a child, I probably drew the sun as a circle with lines radiating from it. Today I know that any approach I take is only one way to represent the sun, although I need to keep in mind that no matter how I choose to paint the sun it will not *be* the sun, only a representation of it. I recently worked on a painting of several people engaged in an outdoor activity they were enjoying a great deal. While I considered a number of ways to paint the sun, I chose to convey it as a circle with lines radiating from it—to convey the childlike fun the adults in my painting were having.

It wouldn't surprise me if someone were to look at that painting and judge that I don't know how to draw a very realistic-looking sun. Quite likely, she would glance at the name on the painting and conclude, correctly, that I am not a well-known artist and that this simple rendition of the sun was the result of a lack of experience or talent. She would, however, be mindlessly neglecting to consider the fact that I chose to paint the sun as I did.

More important, this observer would be closing herself off from understanding why I painted the sun as I did. If I were alongside her, I could point out that Joan Miró painted many suns using circles with lines radiating from them or that David Hockney often runs simple, undulating lines through water to suggest movement, and that their paintings hang in many museums. I would point out that those who do not know much about art often attribute a naïveté to the artist that can be quite mistaken. An awareness that people's behavior may be seen in many different ways can free us to see that what we judge negatively may have been intentional and successful from another perspective.

Put a frog into a pot of water and *gradually* turn up the heat. The frog will keep adjusting to the increasing temperature until, finally, it dies. Put a frog into a pot of *boiling* water, though, and the frog will immediately try to jump out of the pot. We too notice the difference when things change drastically. But when the change is gradual, we accommodate the experience into the frame we are using, even when doing so is to our disadvantage. It doesn't occur to us to consider that the situation, including our behavior or the behavior of other people, might be understood differently from the way we originally framed it. If we did, we could take advantage of cues that are less extreme and notice the "heat" much sooner.

The most important point to understand has already been stated, but its importance bears repeating it. The realization that *all behavior makes sense from the actor's perspective or else the*

actor wouldn't do it makes all negative evaluations of people suspect, and all action based on these evaluations about people
questionable. If we are trying to predict what others will do in
the future and we believe the past is the best predictor, then it
would behoove us to know better what the past action meant to
the actor.

The Effects of Evaluation

*When you show it to someone, if they like it, you're stopped, and if they
dislike it, you're stopped either way.*
ANDREW WYETH

If all evaluation, positive or negative, comes only from a particular state of mind, that does not mean that the consequences of
evaluations are not real. It means that the number of consequences one could enumerate for any action are dependent on
the individual's interest in noting them, and the evaluation of
each of these consequences is dependent on the view taken of it.
Events do not come with evaluations; we impose evaluations on
our experiences and, in so doing, create our experience of the
event.

Consider the following. You're in the midst of drawing and
you make a mistake. There are four possible ways for you to
think about what to do next. One, consider it a mistake and,
since mistakes are intolerable, throw the drawing out. Two, consider the work you've put into the drawing thus far, take another look at the mistake, and conclude you'll live with it.
Three, try to fix the mistake so that everything is just as it was
before you made it. Four, reconsider the mistake and decide to
take advantage of it.

It is the fourth perspective that brings us most of what we
currently value about art, although our culture teaches us to
take only the first three perspectives. Even the seemingly posi-

tive attitude that "every cloud has a silver lining" doesn't quite lead us to trying to take advantage of the situation. The implication of this attitude, instead, is that the something bad will result in something good. We are expected to give up the opportunity to experience the moment, wait for it to pass, and what will result is not just the passing of the bad but the arrival of something good. This is certainly an optimistic viewpoint, but an optimist can be said to be the one who, when surrounded by manure, knows there must be a pony in there somewhere. This is not, of course, the same as taking advantage of the situation. We need to develop an awareness that the very thing which is evaluated as negative is also positive. It is not that there may be five things negative and five positive about it—which surely is better than seeing just the negatives—but that all ten things are both negative and positive, depending on the context we impose on them.

Such cultural expressions are, of course, meant as encouragement and hope, and it is fine to want tomorrow to be better than today and to expect that it will be. When this is what we mean by encouragement and hope, there is no problem. All too often, however, words of hope expressed to people who are feeling bad lead them indirectly to accept those negative feelings and look to tomorrow. They become passive and are led to give up the experience of the moment. Such giving up necessarily follows from the belief that events themselves are good or bad rather than that our views about them make them good or bad. Moreover, these mind-sets implicitly reinforce the idea that events themselves carry inherent evaluations.[2]

One of my students, Sophia Snow, and I conducted a study to see if the way we evaluate activities depends on the context or the label we impose upon them, specifically whether we regard a task as being work or play.[3] We asked participants to perform a series of tasks of increasing difficulty using cartoons from a

Gary Larsen calendar, first sorting them into odd- and even-numbered days, then changing words in order to alter the meanings of the cartoons, and finally sorting them into categories of their own choosing. For half the participants, the task was defined as work, for the other half, it was described as play. When we surveyed the participants about the experience afterward, they reported that they enjoyed the tasks when we labeled them "play" but not when they were labeled "work," despite the fact that the tasks were exactly the same. Twice as often the participants in the "work" group reported that their minds tended to wander as they tried to get through the assignment. These participants were not having fun. But if we change our minds, we don't have to change our tasks. Work needn't be stressful or tedious; if we mindfully engage our work, we don't have to wait until it is over to have fun. Although our culture encourages us to "delay gratification," such waiting is mindless in that it suggests that there is no way to enjoy ourselves in the present. Mere hoping and learning to wait quietly work against our mindfully engaging with the world now.

The cost of evaluation to our inner psychological processes is prodigious. We try to get through the "bad" times; we hesitate to make decisions because the "negative" consequences may be overwhelming. We try to feel better by comparing ourselves with those who are "worse off." We suffer guilt and regret because of the negative consequences we experience or have perpetrated on others. We lie because we see the negative aspects to our behavior and try to hide them from others. Each of these processes—social comparing, regret and guilt, and lying—implies that events are good or bad and that we must learn to accept them as they are and learn to deal with them rather than to question our evaluation of them in the first place.

The implicit message is that there is one yardstick by which to measure not just outcomes but ourselves and others. We look for new explanations only when all else seems to fail. But, as with the frog, by then it may be too little too late. For evaluation to be meaningful, we need to use a common metric. The problems begin when we are oblivious to the fact that many other yardsticks, with very different results inherent in them, could have served as well.[4]

The Evaluative Perspective

Be eager to lend a patient ear to the opinions of others and think long and hard whether whoever finds fault has reason or not to censure you.
LEONARDO DA VINCI

On what basis, then, do we evaluate ourselves and others? Social psychologists working in the field called "attribution theory" have long described the differences in perspective that result from whether one is the actor or the observer of an action.[5] It has been shown that, as actors, we are more likely to attribute our behaviors to the demands or requirements of the situation we are in (what psychologists call a "situational attribution"). We sometimes feel situational constraints keenly, and in retrospect we know quite well why we had to do whatever we did. We also know that in other circumstances we might have behaved differently. By contrast, as observers we are more likely to attribute other people's behavior to their personalities, beliefs, or other internal factors (a "dispositional attribution"). Thus, as observers, we see more clearly the action taken, while the situational constraints affecting those actions are less visible. Often we see the same behavior from different vantage points, but we label it quite differently with respect, primarily, to its evaluative tone. "We" may be interested in getting along with others, for example; "he" may be seen as conforming.

While the research on attribution theory has certainly

yielded important findings, there is another factor that has not yet been examined as fully but that I think needs to be highlighted. Not only do people see different information depending on their vantage point and motivation but people often see the same information differently. In this view, all the behavior of another person may be accounted for by the observer but with a different label, one that carries a very different evaluative tone. Consider, for example, the effect of different labels we might attach to someone: *serious* instead of *grim, flexible* instead of *unpredictable, spontaneous* instead of *impulsive,* or *private* instead of *secretive.* In fact, all human behavior is vulnerable to labels that carry very different evaluative tones. It isn't just that we apply these labels to others. When we act mindlessly, we do so essentially oblivious to the reasons for our behavior, and thus, when we look back at our own behavior, we too may evaluate it as negative.

We often think we understand other people and therefore don't ask others the reasons behind their actions. And because we don't ask, we don't learn that others may have understood their behavior differently than we do. We think we know because we know how we would feel in the same situation, but we imagine that other people are more like us than they really are. Lee Ross has called this the "false consensus effect."[6] We presume that our own behavior makes sense and that any well-adjusted person would act in a similar way.

The false consensus effect is much more common than most of us realize. Experimenters have asked people to predict the opinions and attitudes of others about topics as varied as defense spending, the taste of soup, and what constitutes appropriate behavior in various social situations. Time and again, people overestimated the number of others who would feel or behave as they would. If I falsely assume all of us feel the same and I find out you feel differently, I believe it must be your strange behavior that calls for explanation. Consider that much of the time when people begin their arguments with "most people," they may be making this error. Who are "most people," and how do the arguers know what they'd do? As researchers, we also on occasion make this mistake. We conclude most people would act a particular way, only years later to find out that it was not true for, say, women, people of age twenty-two, people from the East, and so on.

The biggest problem with our tendency toward false consensus is that we turn it on ourselves.[7] When we look back at our own behavior, now from the observer's vantage point, we may see ourselves as having behaved like "one of them." Because, as Kierkegaard observed, we live our lives going forward but understand them looking back, it is important to understand how, as observers, we understand the actions of others. When we look back at our own behavior, we often treat ourselves the same way we do others. Those who are less evaluative of others will be less evaluative of themselves, and the opposite is also true. If we are accomplished at making ourselves feel good when comparing ourselves with others, when we turn things around we become "them," the judged. If, however, we were mindful actors, when we observed our past behaviors we would know why we did as we did and would not accept a negative evaluation.

Consider the following: X is an unpleasant feeling for me. If I do Y, the unpleasantness goes away. Most would argue, then, that it is sensible to do Y. Let's briefly consider drinking in this light. Someone is feeling depressed and emotionally empty. Day after day she drinks, and the pain leaves. Eventually, she may come to think that she has a problem with alcohol. Without knowing that the behavior initially served a purpose, she's likely to suffer self-recrimination. After all, what kind of a person does this to herself? This self-blame, ironically, may lead to more drinking, and so the cycle continues.

From the observer's perspective, "too much" drinking clearly creates unwanted problems for the drinker. The drinker does not say to herself, however, "I have had enough, but I think I'll drink more." The drinker drinks as much as she deems necessary to accomplish whatever her goal may be. Once her goal is accomplished, the drinker does not desire any more alcohol. Her behavior is not irrational when viewed this way. It is undertaken to achieve a state of mind, and it most often accomplishes that goal. Recognizing the sense the action makes gives us more control over the action.

By contrast, when we become observers of our mindless actions, we may become aware of their negative consequences without an understanding of why we did what we did. Looking back as an observer of her actions, the drinker may see that she has caused harm to herself or hurt her loved ones. She probably did not drink to bring about these ends. That is, "going forward" in time, her behavior was not driven by weakness, although looking back without looking for the sense it made, it may seem to have been. For most of us, it is easier to learn something new when we are feeling strong. It would seem, then, that learning how to manage stress or to understand alternative ways of dealing with emptiness, if those are what prompted her drinking, would be easier if the drinker felt good about herself.

We would feel better about ourselves if we saw that, in its own context (that is, from a going-forward perspective), our behavior made sense. With that understanding, self-recrimination makes little sense, and we can instead pursue less costly alternatives for achieving our goals. In her doctoral research, Sharon Popp found that construction workers tend to drink "excessively."[8] Upon questioning them about it, Popp found that, when drinking, they opened up with one another and put their concerns aside. Through these drinking interactions they discovered who they felt they could trust. Trust in their line of work is important, but should they drink or not? In more mundane circumstances, simply asking the question, How may this behavior be sensible? will quickly reveal deeper, reasonable understandings of our own behavior and that of other people. When we see behavior only in the simple frame of right and wrong, this is a question we don't think to ask.

In an experiment that shows the power our frames of reference have over our attitudes, researchers had subjects answer a series of questions that led them to give either introverted answers (for example, What things do you dislike about loud parties?) or extroverted answers (What would you do if you wanted to liven up a party?).[9] After they had finished, the subjects rated themselves on a psychological scale that measures introversion and extroversion. Despite the fact that subjects were randomly assigned to receive one type of question or the other, they tended to see themselves as either introverted or extroverted in accordance with the responses the questions had led them to give.

The power of most great literature and film is that through it we come to see the sense of the actor's behavior even when the actions are to us in some way deplorable. The tension between the two is often the source of the work's power. Consider Vladimir Nabokov's novel *Lolita*. If we could feel only disgust for Humbert, there would be no problem. After all, grown men are not supposed to become sexually aroused and active with adolescent girls. Nabokov's skill reveals itself in drawing us inside Humbert's character, so that we cannot so easily dismiss him. In Shakespeare's play, we do not see only that Hamlet killed his stepfather; that would not be interesting. Instead, we are led to see how we could have made the same awful mistake. We all tend to enjoy literature and film more when we can identify with the characters. Simply being observers barely justifies the price we've paid for the popcorn. But great works may let us identify with the protagonist and then take us places we thought we would never go.

I am advocating what I know is a radical position. Individual differences are primarily differences in experience, not differences in individuals. You and I each have our hand on a hot radiator. I have to remove my hand more quickly than you do. Are you braver or more able to endure pain? Not really. If you felt what I felt, you would remove your hand when I removed mine.

I see ten horses running at full gallop toward us. I'm pleased they are coming to say hello, but everyone else runs for cover. They claim I'm in denial; I compare myself with them and wonder what is wrong with me. Alternatively, they stay and I run, and we all understand I'm a coward. If our experience has led us to think the horses would hurt us, running is sensible. If our experience has led us to think horses are friendly, we stay to greet them. Some of us have learned one, some the other, and so we behave differently. By presuming my behavior doesn't make sense, you don't get to learn that horses may be friendly.

It is interesting that our culture provides us with norms that lead us to misunderstand our own and other people's behavior. If we commit an "error," say we do something in haste and it doesn't turn out well, we might become contrite or indignant at the reaction of others. Which of those attitudes we choose to take might well depend on whether we tell ourselves that "patience is a virtue" or that "the early bird catches the worm." We may think we should have been satisfied with the outcome if we accept that "a bird in the hand is worth two in the bush," or not, if we imagine that "nothing ventured is nothing gained." On another occasion, we might imagine we were cowardly in not acting if we believe in "an eye for an eye" instead of the need to "turn the other cheek." Even our most mundane behaviors are hard to pin down; is it "clothes make the man" or "you can't judge a book by its cover"?

The fact is that we can either always make sense out of our behavior or take ourselves to task, and our culture provides some of our evidence for whichever we choose. The problem is that most of us, much of the time, don't realize there is a choice to be made. Often blind to our motives, we tend to feel even more culpable or blameful when we call to mind any of these, or similar, refrains that suggest we should have known better. Just as each individual behavior has an individual perspective that lends reason to the action taken, so does the opposite behavior.

Discrimination Is Not Evaluation

Good art is not what it looks like, but what it does to us.
Roy Adzak

It is important to note that *we can be discriminating without being evaluative.* Noticing new things about the world is the essence of mindfulness. Unquestioningly accepting a single-minded evaluation of what we notice is mindless. Our culture is replete with examples of mindless evaluation. Unfortunately, it is hard to conjure up examples of a more mindful stance, since we take an evaluative component as an essential part of our beliefs. Without knowing whether they are good or bad, after all, how would we know whether to approach or avoid ideas, people, places, and things? Yet in accepting evaluation rather than mindful discrimination as essential, we set ourselves up for the experience of feeling inadequate. By mindlessly attaching this evaluative component to our beliefs, we become victims of our mind-sets. We experience this reactivity only when things go "wrong." These are the times we try to change; yet these are the times we are least equipped to do so.

With the awareness that we are responsible for our evaluations, we are more likely to use them in conditional ways. In this way we can stay responsive to our circumstances rather than become reactive to them, as absolute evaluations lead us to be.

The Danger of Compliments

The important thing is never to let oneself be guided by the opinion of one's contemporaries; to continue steadfastly on one's way without letting oneself be either defeated by failure or diverted by applause.
GUSTAV MAHLER

If someone compliments us, what should our reaction be and how should we understand it? If we are extremely pleased, for instance, our pleasure might suggest a certain amount of uncertainty about our level of skill. It also suggests a degree of vulnerability. Imagine that someone whose opinion you respect told you that you were great at spelling three-letter words. Chances are, if you're over ten years old, you would not be moved by the compliment. You know that spelling three-letter words is easy, so the feedback is unimportant to you. Now imagine that the same person told you that the way you pronounce vowels is extraordinary. Again, you'd be unlikely to be very moved. This time you're not taken in by the compliment because the issue probably doesn't matter much to you. In both cases, because you were not being tested by it, the compliment was unimportant.

I can imagine a situation in which I win an award for my work, and while pleased, I am not convinced I deserved it more than others in my field. I won't accept the unbridled wisdom of those who conferred this honor on me. Of course I'm pleased, but I recognize the uncertainty or chance that goes into receiving any such honor. The judges, in fact, could have different views about my work than I do, they could have used different criteria upon which to judge it, or they might highlight or ignore different understandings of what my work means. As a result, winning the award may mean more to me than being complimented on being able to spell three-letter words, but it does not confirm that I am a worthwhile psychologist, let alone a worthwhile person.

If I accept the award as confirmation that I'm worthwhile, what happens when I don't win some award in the future? At that point, asking how these evaluations are made feels like I'm lying to myself—rationalizing why I didn't win. If as a general rule I recognize that whether I win the award or not, these things are determined by well-meaning but not omniscient judges, how will I feel if I'm overlooked? I'm not likely to be upset. I am not busying myself in rationalizing being passed over because the genuine understanding I have about evaluations precedes the outcome and is not a result of it. I am not lying to myself; I hold the view that evaluations are subjective. If I hold this view, what is my yardstick for feeling like a worthwhile person? There is no yardstick. I am, therefore I am worthwhile.

While it would be nice if we were so enlightened at all times, it's easy to get caught by compliments. When I first painted Nancy's dog, Sparky, I knew I was sure to get a compliment from her. I love Sparky, and it turns out that I am somehow able to capture what I'm told is his essence, whatever that means. And so enjoying the compliment, I kept on painting him. Then Anthony said, "Okay, you've mastered Sparky. How about painting your own dogs, Gus and Girlie?"

I was actually afraid to try. Why? What would have happened if I discovered that all I could paint was Sparky? Most of our fears are just this silly. How would I or the world be different if it turned out that I could paint only Sparky? There was no real cost, and yet I was afraid. Despite the fear, I took what felt like a risk and painted the other two dogs. It worked; I've got their "essences" too. Now I'm afraid to try any other dog. It's outrageous. I could have said to myself, after having successfully painted Sparky, that I enjoy and am not bad at painting dogs. Instead, the next step for me was believing that I didn't know if I could paint my own dogs. What would I really lose if I couldn't paint a "good" dog?

I once tried to paint my friends Anthony and Linda's big black Lab. The result looked nothing like him. I concluded I couldn't paint black dogs. Anthony, trying to be helpful, told me to paint a very big white dog and then paint it black. It didn't help. I know there is not much cost in trying and all that I'd have to accept is that I can't do everything right away. But I already know that, so why is it that, each time I learn it, it feels like new advice to me? Why do I fear the insult? Why do I need the compliment? I tried painting two large brown dogs (which turned out quite mediocre) and a small dog looking at them. Anthony saw the painting, and before we could discuss the problems with the big dogs, he looked at the small one and exclaimed, "Ellen, you're the Leonardo of the small dog." He marveled at the fact that, anatomically, my small dogs are wrong, but still they are, as he says, "perfect." After we talked through my approach to the two big dogs, I tried again, with better results. I'm getting there, but the journey from small dog to large dog could have been much more rewarding if I had simply put evaluation aside.

One day I was at the Provincetown Art Museum, and I noticed several paintings that were coming off the wall from a member's show. I thought some of my paintings were just as good, and I decided to enter the next show. A few days later, I returned to the museum to submit one of my paintings for the next juried show, and I noticed immediately that the work being submitted was much more sophisticated than the paintings in the previous exhibition. I hesitated, but having filled out the entry papers, I couldn't get my painting back without a long story and no small embarrassment. Reluctantly, I entered the show. I told myself that if my entry were rejected, which I expected, it would mean only that a few people did not like it as well as they liked other works, not that my work had no merit.

When I called a week later to make arrangements to pick up the painting, I was told it was one of twenty works selected from a hundred artists' submissions. I was thrilled. That was fine, but I would have been better off had I realized that being accepted did not mean that my painting had any inherent value. It meant that, at this time and for a variety of reasons, the people in the equation—the jury—liked my work. I was pleased by the compliment, but by not taking it too seriously, I would have protected myself from the emotional roller coaster that was to come. A new show was announced. Could I do it again? Now I was too afraid to test myself.

We all need to keep in mind that evaluations are made by people based on their experience and their own needs. They are not handed down from the heavens. The assumption that absolute criteria exist can reasonably lead to our being afraid to act, to giving up, after even one rejection, or even after our first success.

Behaviorist literature tells us that there are positive and negative reinforcements and positive and negative forms of punishment. Positive reinforcement is the presentation of a positive stimulus, for example, a compliment. Negative reinforcement is the cessation of an aversive stimulus—if someone is always insulting you and now you do something and no insult follows, that behavior will be negatively reinforced. Reinforcement enhances the response leading to it; whether it is positive or negative, reinforcement feels good. Conversely, punishment is meant to stop the behavior that leads to it. Positive punishment is the presentation of an aversive stimulus, such as an insult. The interesting but less well-known type of punishment is negative punishment—the cessation of a positive stimulus. (Time out from compliments can be punishing.) Because compliments feel so good, we are not inclined to look much beyond them. Because compliments may help control us, there is little motivation for others to see their costs to us. Compliments and insults help keep us in an evaluative frame of mind. But evaluating the self takes one out of the experience; self becomes object rather than actor. Ironically, with less experience, there is less of a self to evaluate. As we will soon discuss, if we don't take the compliment, we're not vulnerable to the insult.

It may be that we stay evaluative because positive evaluation helps us feel good in the short run. As soon as we agree to accept a positive evaluation as reason to feel good about ourselves, however, we open the door for the damaging consequences of perceived failure. Surely depression, suicide, or just feeling bad about life all result in whole or in part from an evaluative stance.

Once, while in Mexico, I began a painting of a woman reclining on a bed while reading and eating chocolates. I stopped to prepare for a dinner party and left the painting without having finished her face. When I returned I looked at the painting anew and liked it just the way it was, which should have been all I needed to be satisfied with it. But then I showed it to a former art teacher who had been complimentary about my work some months earlier. Of my new, prized painting he said, "It's good, almost art." Dejected, I put away the canvas and didn't look at it again till several months later. My emotions went up and down, up and down, until I realized that before I had started taking compliments too seriously, painting had been all up for me. Moreover, I realized that compliments were even taking over my painting. For a while I had been using one color over and over because people told me they liked that color. Then one day a friend told me to "lose the color for a while, Ellen." Now I'm choosing colors freely once again.

All of us, when we look at art in museums, can see how many disparate styles there are. But we act in our creative lives as if there is one single standard. The same variety exists for furniture, fashion, music, weaving, or anything else for that matter. I have not infrequently gone into a clothing store, tried something on, and asked a salesperson for an "opinion" that I take as fact, without realizing that I don't even like what the salesperson is wearing. We spend much of our lives looking for right answers and in doing so give up control.

The work of Margarett Sargent, a famous Boston artist, sculptor, and painter of the 1930s, was more emotional than that of most of her contemporaries. She produced a wonderful painting, entitled *Beyond Good and Evil,* that suggests Sargent sought to escape from the daily judgments of right and wrong. But she found it difficult to be accepted as an artist and, instead, escaped into alcohol. Dorothy Adlow wrote in 1938 of the women artists of the time: "They have generally been made to feel like barbarians and intruders by the patrician arbiters of taste."[10] Professional male artists decried the loss of standards as several young women—Polly Thayer, Aimee Lamb, and Margarett Sargent among them—forged a new way of painting, and thus seeing. They struggled to put aside ideas of right and wrong. But that was then, and as it is said, this is now. From representational art to conceptual art or, in fashion, from hemlines above the knee to hemlines only inches from the floor, we can see that the idea of "right" answers is questionable.

If you try and don't succeed, you can feel you are a failure or you conclude that you simply haven't yet found an effective path to success. James Joyce's famous book *The Dubliners* was rejected by twenty-two publishers before it became a classic. Gertrude Stein submitted poems to editors for about twenty years before one was accepted. Fred Astaire and the Beatles were also initially told they didn't have it. The list goes on and on; we don't need to add ourselves to it.

Freeing Ourselves from Evaluation

Most supposed aesthetic absolutes prove relative under pressure.
JOHN GARDNER

If we can only learn to think mindfully about how evaluation works on us, we won't have to be held hostage by it. When we are evaluative, we confuse the stability of our mind-sets with the stability of the underlying phenomenon. We think the world is stable, but it's really changing. It's our mind-sets that don't change, and our evaluations are always based on the past. That's mindless, of course. We evaluate information and put it away in our minds, then don't have it available to us to use later, when we, or the context in which we find ourselves, changes. When we accept an evaluation, in essence we're saying that we don't need to be there, we've given up choice. When confronted with a clear evaluation, we can just do what's dictated. When we're hard on ourselves, it's because we have a very rigid sense of what we're supposed to be doing. We run from doubt because we feel we should know. Ironically, people want choice yet are afraid of uncertainty. But the truth is, *If there is no doubt, there is no choice.* If we recognize that doubt allows choice, we can become mindfully creative. This is a very different kind of choice making than we are used to having. It is a liberating kind of choice, unlike the choice we face from evaluation, which is immobilizing because it rests on the implicit assumption that, without doubt, there is a correct choice.[11]

If you undergo a personal renaissance, you are able to choose the context yourself. Your behavior is, oddly enough, more consistent but based on internal criteria. Evaluations are closely tied to contexts—what's in at the moment. What I don't like today, I may or may not like tomorrow. A personal renaissance makes you more confident, not that you can do this thing but that you *want* to do this thing. You can say to yourself, "I'm now confident that I will enjoy doing it regardless of the final product or the outcome."

There's a not knowing that leads us to accept external evaluation. Once we appreciate that what we did makes sense or else we would not have done it, we're not held hostage to our own or anyone else's negative evaluation. Now you can show your latest drawing to anyone. If we know our internal rationale, we don't need to accept those of others.

A personal renaissance is an internal life that's not cut off from the external world; instead, the external is food for our internal lives. *Once we've achieved a personal renaissance, we enjoy the excitement as though everything is at stake but we have the awareness that nothing is.* We not only listen to what others say, but we can actually hear their comments nondefensively.

The Pleasure of Not Stopping

A painting is never finished—it simply stops in interesting places.
PAUL GARDNER

One of the great pleasures of giving up evaluation in favor of a personal renaissance is the joy of knowing that things don't have a fixed beginning, middle, or end. If you don't know where you are going, you keep doing something because you enjoy it. You keep doing it, making choices, and noticing the consequences until it's pleasing to you and you *want* to stop.

It's not that I'm indiscriminate, but I like most of my paintings. If I didn't like one, I would have continued working on it until I did. But I also like them for the experience of having done them, of having learned something in doing them. That sounds like an evaluation, and it is in some sense, but it relies on a relationship between who I am and these things that I've created. When that's congruent, it feels satisfying. That's a very different kind of evaluation from one that implicitly suggests stability and external criteria. It's one that doesn't hold us hostage. At any point we can choose to engage in something else. We can stop painting the painting, playing the suite, or composing the poem, but our decision needn't be based on an evaluation of the worth of the painting, the music, or the writing. I can appreciate it for what it is and move on.

Personal growth is marked by being responsive rather than reactive to the world around us. When we are less reactive, we are able to make more choices. When we make more choices, we become less reactive. By contrast, we find ourselves stuck in place when we get attached to situations because of the evaluations we make. When we open up and see that evaluations can change—that schools, eras, contexts aren't fixed—our awareness can lead us to a mindful state.

Our culture wants us to end things by evaluating them. When it's good enough to be called over, move on to the next thing. Finishing, however, need not be a criterion for beginning something else. Finishing relies on an assumption (that is, an evaluation) of what the final product *is* and *should be.*

A mindful life doesn't define engagement as having a clear beginning, middle, and end. It's harder to begin something new if we focus on what it is going to be, and in doing so cut ourselves off from the possibilities that arise in the doing. When we do stop, on one level the engagement may be over—we put down our paintbrush—but that needn't be the final result. When we see an activity as complete, we often don't think of returning to it, although to do so may be fun. For most of us, even when we intend to return to an activity, getting back into it often feels more difficult than it needs to because we struggle to find a starting point. Let me suggest another way. Instead of hurrying to "finish" some part of the painting, book, or piece of music we are working on, leave off in the middle. Now we'll know exactly where to begin again and reengagement will be much easier. For example, if I'm painting a person who wears glasses and I don't rush to finish painting his glasses, when I return to the painting it's easy to get started. I just get ready to start painting the glasses. Of course, now that I'm reengaged, I might even decide not to paint him or her with glasses.

Think of growing plants and raising children. We don't expect those experiences ever to be completed, do we? Beginnings, middles, and ends are laden with evaluation.

"It doesn't matter how a thing starts off," the film director David Lynch told *The New York Times*, "what matters is paying attention to where the ideas are leading you. Because when you think you're leading them, that's when you get into trouble."[12]

The Myth of Inaction

A beautiful thing never gives so much pain as does failing to hear and see it.
MICHELANGELO

If it is good—approach. If it is bad—avoid. The action is clear. But what happens when we recognize that it is neither good nor bad? Would giving up evaluation lead us to inaction?

Consider the phenomenon that many of us call a midlife crisis. At some point in life, many people come to realize that nothing has intrinsic meaning. There are three responses to this moment. Those who do not successfully emerge from this belief stay depressed and cynical at the meaninglessness of it all. Some ignore this belief and proceed as if they never had it, although all the while it lurks in the background. Finally, there are those who accept that everything is equally meaningless or meaningful. This last group is the most likely to stay situated in a self-constructed, meaningful present—a personal renaissance.

A person can take action falsely believing that the action will result in a single desirable outcome and repeatedly suffer surprise and disappointment if it fails. That same person can come to see that the action may not in fact lead to the outcome or that the outcome may not be desirable anyway, and thus decide not to take any action. But a third option also presents itself. It is typically more satisfying to do something than to do nothing. Because we know evaluations are products of our minds, we can eliminate them and take action without fear of negative evaluation. Action is the way we get to experience ourselves. And so, *we act not to bring about an outcome but to bring about ourselves.*

If they could be assured that their action would not result in negative outcomes, would people hesitate to act? People prefer action to inaction. In an elevator, we go to press the button for our floor even if it's already lit. The fear of inaction has hidden in it the evaluative belief that making the "wrong" decision may be costly. Recent research we have conducted, in fact, shows that mindfulness leads to quicker, not more prolonged, decision making. People in our study who were taught to reframe positive as negative, and vice versa, released the hold evaluations had on them and made their decisions more, not less, quickly.[13] Giving up our evaluative tendencies does not seem to lead to inaction.

This is not to say that "inaction" is necessarily bad. Typically we see inaction as the absence of a particular action. That is, we don't make the phone call, buy the item, attend the event. We need not, however, see ourselves as inactive in these situations but rather as actively pursuing another course, even if it's actively "doing nothing." If we realized this, we might be less afraid of giving up the illusion of evaluative stability.

The Power of Mindfulness

I am enough of an artist to draw freely upon my imagination. Imagination is more important than knowledge. Knowledge is limited. Imagination encircles the world.
ALBERT EINSTEIN

Isn't the answer to most problems simply that we need to think positively? I'm often asked whether that isn't the true path to learning to live a richer, more creative life. It might seem that the power of positive thinking is all we need, but I don't think so and positive thinking may not be a match for the power of a mindful approach to life. Moreover, if a positive evaluation is real then logically so too must be a negative evaluation. If mindful, we are neither positive nor negative; we just are.

I've been studying happiness for more than thirty years since my early work in cognitive behavior therapy. Even in situations that would seem truly negative, a more mindful view has been shown to be of benefit. For example, we examined a mindful approach to major surgery.[14] People about to undergo major surgery are all too aware of the negative aspects that can be ascribed to this event. In this experiment, we taught one group of subjects to add to their understanding a very different positive view of their hospital experience. As compared with other patients given different communications, our mindful subjects became happier, experienced less stress, and required less medication. This is not the same as convincing people that what they thought was negative is *really* positive. Rather, it is convincing them that they can choose how they want to appraise the situation.

It would also seem to follow that to be positive would be to accept positive statements by others, that is, compliments, but as we've seen, to do so sets us up for negative punishment. If being positive means we should be grateful that we are not as badly off as others might be, then such gratitude comes at the expense of others. Most important, if we teach people to be positive, we may unintentionally teach them to continue to tie evaluation to events, ideas, and people, and thus promote mindlessness.

When mindful, rather than simply positive, we may find solutions to the problems that made us feel incompetent. We may avert the danger not yet arisen. By becoming less judgmental, we are likely to come to value other people and ourselves. All told, it would seem that being mindful would lead us to be at peace with ourselves, obviating the need for learning how to be positive.

Thus, while there is certainly likely to be a higher correlation between positive evaluations and well-being, positive evaluations make negative evaluations appear independent of us. By seeing ourselves as fortunate when we have positive experiences, we implicitly deny the understanding that outcomes are products of our minds, and thus suggest that there is still potential negativity one may have to confront. Thus positive evaluations may implicitly rob us of control. By contrast, the mindful individual comes to recognize that each outcome is potentially simultaneously positive and negative (as is each aspect of each outcome) and that choices can be made with respect to our affective experience. Thus, the mindful individual is likely to choose to be positive and will experience both the advantages of positivity and the advantages of perceived control. In so doing, that person will have less reason to resist desires to take up new challenges.

People often tell those who are being negative that they ought to be positive. It is as if they presume negative people see a choice and decide to make themselves miserable by choosing the negative view. Then, in a well-meaning way, many provide positive alternatives to help the negative people feel better. The problem with this approach is that a self-generated view is likely to feel more real than a view generated by someone else. Now the negative person not only feels the impact of whatever the negative view was but may also feel incompetent for having been less able to see the situation differently. People see what they see and then act accordingly. Whether it is positive or negative, people overwhelmingly take the evaluation as part of the thing being evaluated rather than as a mind-set we attach to it. More effective advice may be to encourage people to view the situation mindfully. By generating multiple consequences that have personal meaning, the individual is back in control and can then choose to attend to the positive consequences, if evaluation feels necessary.

A wise and respected judge was in court one day. The first man made his case, and the judge said, "You're right." The second man cried out, "You haven't heard my side." The judge listened as he spoke and then said, "You're right." A third man stood up and said, "They can't both be right, they are saying opposite things." To which the judge replied, "You're right."

There is no behavior we would all agree is wrong across all contexts; nor is there a way of acting that we would agree is always correct. Killing is wrong if it means taking the life of an innocent other, perhaps right if it leads to saving one's own children from serious harm. Helping is important except perhaps when it is intended to make the helper feel holier than thou or the recipient feel "less than." Clearly, there is a degree of relativity that most of us already accept. Because each of our behaviors can be couched in opposite ways on an evaluative scale—has a good-bad dimension—we tend to do what we want to do and find the moral reasons for it after the fact. With a moral reason in hand, we emerge thinking of ourselves as having a clear sense of right and wrong. We not only act differently in different situations but also act differently in the same situation and label our behavior differently.

Am I a moral relativist? Yes and no. Yes, when it comes to judging our actions, no, when it comes to what would be the products of those actions if we gave up our judgment. That is, if all of us were living mindful lives, I believe the very wrongs we try to right would not occur. Rape that results from powerlessness, theft that results from the belief that owning any particular object makes one a worthwhile person, and so on, would have no place. These are truly serious matters. Despite the air of seriousness we attach to most of our own mundane actions, a closer look makes them seem superficial by comparison.

Our evaluative judgments often lead us to take ourselves too seriously. By taking ourselves too seriously, and everything personally, we actually keep ourselves from becoming personally involved. It is to our advantage to be personally involved but not to make things personal. By making everything mindfully personal, that is to take things seriously enough to notice the world around us, we are able to experience the world without making it be about ourselves. We take *it*, not *ourselves* seriously.

4

The Mindfulness of Mistakes

In the brush doing what it's doing, it will stumble on what one couldn't do by oneself.
ROBERT MOTHERWELL

NOT LONG AFTER I STARTED PAINTING, THERE WAS A SALE ON ART supplies at a local discount store. One of my students happened upon it and called me to see if I wanted anything. I wasn't home at the time, but she managed to reach my friend Nancy, who right away told her to buy out the store and she would make the supplies a gift to me. When I came home that evening, I found a number of very large canvases, which seemed to have been the bulk of the items on sale, apparently because many people are hesitant to attempt large paintings. I've painted on very large canvases and very small ones, but to my surprise, when people see the large ones, regardless of whether they like the paintings, they seem to feel it was quite bold of me to paint them. Boldness was not an issue—I had the canvases and so I used them.

I thought to ask several of my artist friends about their experience, and they explained the differences between working on large paintings and small ones and the challenges each presented. In thinking about it, I realized that, had I learned these differences in advance, I probably would have not attempted the very large or the very small paintings that I had. I would not have felt my strokes were bold enough for the former or delicate enough for the latter. I didn't have to take a course to see that the size of the brush that works best is related to the size of the canvas. If I used a very small brush on the large canvas, the painting would take me forever, and it's easy to imagine the effect of a very large brush on the very small canvas. But, since I didn't know the rules, I just went ahead, unafraid of the mistakes I might or might not have been making.

Discovering for myself the differences between painting on large and small canvases was part of the fun. It also meant that I still approach choices about size as opportunities to learn. I'm not wedded, for instance, to the idea that brush and canvas size need to be related in all cases. Mindlessly holding to that rule, I believe, could result in a mistake. More important, it could result in an opportunity lost—the bold small painting or the deliberate oversize one.

Most of us fail to engage in creative endeavors as meaningfully as we might, or even decline to involve ourselves in them altogether, because the risk of making mistakes is too great. What does "making a mistake" mean, and why does the urge to avoid mistakes have so much power over us?

If we don't begin with a rigid plan, it is hard to make a mistake. Our rather mindless aversion to mistakes is rooted in our belief in plans, that is, in our expectation that we should execute a plan we had previously set, with no deviations. Ultimately, this is a defeating mind-set, one that does not take advantage of what our present circumstances offer us. Mistakes, if we are attentive to them, can help us tune in to the present and allow us more mindfully to pursue our desires rather than our rigid plans. Mistakes are signals that we went off our predetermined course, but they can present us with choices we may not otherwise have recognized.[1]

If we were not so prone to evaluate unexpected outcomes as

single-mindedly negative, we would not be faced with the problem of how to cope with mistakes in the first place. I once returned to my house after a heavy rain and found that I had left my windows open. Instead of berating myself, I decided I was glad for the help in damp-mopping the floors. There was an event—it rained—and an outcome—water on the floors. I didn't use it as a means for self-evaluation or take the opportunity for self-condemnation for having left the windows open when rain seemed likely. Rather, I took the opportunity to make use of the outcome. One could certainly argue that this example is trivial, but researchers have found that these small, daily "annoyances" are what cause most of our stress. And it is also the case that we have the most control over our reactions to these kinds of occurrences.

Our taking control of the everyday can, in fact, have large effects. In 1945 Richard James, a naval engineer, was conducting experiments with tension springs for the military. During one experiment, one of the springs accidentally fell to the floor and began to "walk." Although the spring was unsuitable for the Navy's purposes, James took it home to his wife, Betty, and asked her if she thought it had potential. Betty's vision for the spring, which she called a Slinky, as we all know, made toy history.

Mistakes, like all evaluations, are context-dependent. In one context a mistake is an error, while in another it can be a surprise advantage. Others have spoken to the dual nature of mistakes but typically in reference to grander events. We all have heard that "there is opportunity in chaos." What we may not know, however, is why that is so. I propose the answer is that mistakes may provoke mindfulness, and perhaps, as such, we ought to welcome and not just tolerate them.

The Nature of Mistakes

Mistakes are the portals of discovery.
JAMES JOYCE

If we are to learn to value mistakes, we must first learn something of their nature. Compare a handmade Oriental rug with one that is machine-made. The machine-made rug is clearly more perfect, yet the handmade rug is far more valuable. It's not just the hours of labor that make it so; it's the inherent appeal of the handmade rug that makes it worth more to us. One way to understand why this is so is to realize that the mindfulness of the handmade rug is visible to us through the errors that were made during its construction. We could note that the things that make an artist's work interesting to others are often the very mistakes most of us are trying to avoid. In fact, what may make any of our activities interesting to us are our mistakes. Turning on a light or pressing a button in an elevator was fun when we were very young. But once the behavior is mastered, it produces little enjoyment.

I found this to be true while painting. I once painted a canvas of two women, one centered and the other to one side, in the background. When I stepped back to look at it, I wasn't satisfied with the painting, and so I decided to paint it over, intending to block it out entirely. I didn't, however, put enough paint on the brush, which also was too wet from sitting in a coffee can full of water. Instead of obliterating the painting, I covered the entire canvas with a thin whitewash. When I turned back to the canvas, armed with another brush, now "correctly" full of paint and an intent more fitting to house painting than to art, I looked once more. It was mysterious. All of the "errors" that had led me to want to wash away the painting now added to its appeal. I liked what I saw. It wasn't great, but still, I found it held my interest. When I showed it to Anthony, he suggested that I paint something over the wash so it would look as though it had been deliberate. Intrigued, I painted a glass of red wine right in the middle of the canvas and smiled at my "deliberate" accomplishment.

When I was in the hospital not long ago nursing a broken ankle, several staff members watched while I painted. It's interesting how quickly we can become experts. One of the aides looked into my room with envy so often that I insisted she paint with me. I told her the fun doesn't begin until you make your first error. She didn't believe me, but I kept asking her, "Did you make a mistake yet?" After a little while she replied that she had in fact made a mistake and wanted to know how to fix it. I told her to look away from the picture for a moment. "To make an error," I suggested, "simply means to have done something that we had not previously planned to do." After she looked back at her painting, I told her to complete it, incorporating the mistake. She did so, and she loved the painting, as did the nurses who put it on display.

Mistakes, in this way, encourage mindfulness. By being dissuaded from mindlessly pursuing a plan, we can place ourselves squarely in the present and create something new, outside the plan. Indeed, if we set out to paint a particular couch in a particular way without varying from the script, how would that be different from painting by numbers? Once we question where our plan came from, we will recognize that it was just based on an earlier decision, with all the uncertainty endemic to decisions. The looser our plan, the more room for creating something new, which is a far more rewarding activity. As the writer André Gide once said, "One does not discover new lands without consenting to lose sight of the shore for a very long time."

We don't often imagine that the best-known artists value mistakes. It is said that Miró was fanatically neat, but when asked how he started a painting, he replied, "Sometimes I start with brushes that are dirty. I wipe them across a new canvas. . . . I like old brushes, uneven, flattened out, that produce 'accidents.' An old brush has vitality . . . a life of its own." Of a clean canvas, he said, "I begin to dirty it a bit, I splash it with turpentine, rub it with my paint-stained hands. I even walk on it . . . or I begin with a piece of paper that I crumple up. . . . If the canvas is just new and clean, it's cold, it doesn't excite me."[2]

I've been told that the hardest thing for some artists to know is when to stop working on a painting. There is a scene in the movie *Pollock* where a reporter from *Life* magazine asks Jackson Pollock how he knows when a painting is finished and he responds, "How do you know when you're finished making love?" I'm not sure that his answer is much help for anyone who genuinely wants to know, but it does highlight the idea that we just know if we are there to find out. Alternatively, we could rely on our plan and stop where it dictates stopping—regardless of the sense stopping or going forward might now make. Certainly our work can never match exactly the images we hold in our minds as plans for that work. Rarely will we be able to make it just as we thought it would be. But by struggling to do so, we often miss what it is—or could have been—if we had just left it alone, without trying to *fix* our mistakes, and went somewhere new and off plan. Once we make a "mistake," it may be easier to give up mindlessly following our plan and go forward. When we feel we've made a mistake, we often act as if the original plan had been perfect. We weren't sure at step one, so why be so distressed at step two? "Should this painting have Girlie or Gus in it?" I might ask with some uncertainty. I decide to include Girlie. I make a "mistake" and paint her ears too big. Knowing I wasn't sure what dog to paint in the first place makes it easier now to change it to Gus—my dog with the funny ears.

Erich Lessing/Art Resource, NY

There is a wonderful painting by Jean-Auguste-Dominique Ingres, *La Grande Odalisque,* that demonstrates how mistakes don't really detract from our appreciation of art. If you look carefully, you will notice that the woman's thigh is at least the size of her torso, not a proportion we find very often in the real world. Still, she looks right, sensual and not grotesque. *La Grande Odalisque* is a beautiful painting, not at all flawed by this "error." The woman's body is different from bodies in the real world but no less representative of them or their beauty.

Édouard Manet was often the subject of derision by critics of his time. He was actually accused of incompetence for his painting *A Bar at the Folies-Bergère,* in which he made no attempt to relate the reflections in the mirror behind the bar with the scene he placed in front of the bar. The man in the top hat approaching the barmaid in the upper-right-hand corner of the mirror would, in reality, have to be standing with his back to us in front of the bar. The barmaid's reflection should be placed more toward the center of the mirror, rather than to the right. The critics' scorn of this painting was so great that a newspaper caricature at the time "fixed" the mistakes. But these errors, if that's what they are, haven't detracted from our appreciation of the painting at all; they only add to its meaning.

Upon viewing *Les Demoiselles d'Avignon,* a man asked Picasso why he didn't paint women the way they really looked. When Picasso asked him how women really look, the man produced a photo of his wife. Picasso looked at it and said that he now understood: Women are small, and black and white, and flat.

If we know just where we are going we can't go anywhere new. Mistakes not only set the stage for a mindful approach to the work at hand but also reveal our individuality. When we all act according to the same plan, our final products are likely to look the same, just as machine-made rugs do. Our "errors," by contrast, stand a chance to be both unique and interesting. The difference between a line drawn with a ruler and one drawn by hand is that, in the latter, the individual shines through.

Recently, Brianna Cummings, Yulia Steshenko, Noah Eisen-

The Samuel Courtauld Trust, Courtauld Institute of Art Gallery, London

kraft, and Shauna Campbell, members of our lab, and I tested the notion that mistakes can lead to better final outcomes.[3] We gave participants paper and pens, asking them to draw a picture of an animal. Before they began to draw they were told either that if they made a mistake, they should see it as a cue to be in the moment and to incorporate the mistake into their drawing or that it was human to make a mistake. Some of the subjects were then forced to make a "mistake" in the middle of their drawing. (We did this by telling them they were supposed to draw a different animal after they had begun drawing. For example, as soon as we recognized that someone had begun a bear, we would interrupt her and tell her she was to draw an animal that lived in the water.) Participants worked in pen so they weren't able to erase their "mistakes." We also conducted the experiment with a third group, who completed their drawings without interference.

When they had finished, we asked all to complete a questionnaire about their artistic experience, whether they enjoyed the task, and how they would rate their drawings. The group that incorporated their mistakes into their drawings reported that they enjoyed the activity more than the others. We also had judges rate how much they preferred each drawing. The judges preferred the drawings by the group that had to find a way to incorporate their mistakes.

We conducted a similar study where, instead of drawing, we had participants write essays. Again, one group was told to incorporate any mistakes they made into their essay. Another was simply told it was human to make a mistake. We next primed the mistake groups with questions about what they had had for breakfast. Then we read aloud instructions to each group, asking them to write an essay about "mourning," but because they had been primed with thoughts of "breakfast," they instead wrote about "morning." Halfway through, we gave them a questionnaire that asked them if they found it difficult to write about mourning, thereby revealing their mistake. Not only did participants who incorporated their mistakes into the essay later report that they enjoyed the activity more than the other groups did, the judges who rated the completed essays preferred the "mindful mistake" essays to the others—even to those of the group that didn't make a mistake.

Our fear of mistakes is so strong that it often leads us to feel inadequate and to undertake a pointless review of the past instead of looking to the present and future. Imagine that you are in a hurry and want to make a cup of tea. When you reach for the only clean cup on the shelf, it drops and cracks. Many of us would immediately comment on how clumsy we are and, after realizing there weren't any clean cups, forget about having tea. But, imagine that on another occasion you go to get a cup but notice that the only one available is cracked down the side. It seems to me that, in the latter situation, people are more likely to consider that they may use the cup anyway or how they might, albeit temporarily, fix it so they can use it, or look for an alternative.

In another study we presented people with just this situation and others like it. We asked some of them to imagine that they had mistakenly broken the cup, while others were told that the cup was broken beforehand. Both groups were asked what they would do about getting their tea. Those who were allowed to accept the broken cup as a fait accompli, without having to deal with it as a mistake they had made, came up with a number of creative solutions for the problem. The mistake group generally did not. No one in the "non-mistake" group gave up and didn't have anything to drink, although several in the "mistakes" group did. This was true for several scenarios we tested.

James Joyce said, "A man of genius makes no mistakes." Perhaps there is more to that statement than first meets the mind. Ingeniously using our mistakes, or even learning to ignore them, *can* enhance our creative results. Perhaps we should all take a lesson from Robert Frost. When he wrote poems that didn't work to his satisfaction, he called them "exercises." That is genius. Exercises carry with them the idea of improvement. Mistakes, by contrast, suggest incompetence.

When we are first learning to do anything, we ought to expect to make mistakes and we should see our mistakes as steps along the way to competence. We encourage children not to expect perfection, especially at first. Why, even as adults, if we've never tried to paint, or write, or play an instrument, should we start by expecting perfection?

Mistakes and Rules

Writing is finally a series of permissions you give yourself to be expressive in certain ways. To invent. To leap. To fly. To fall.
SUSAN SONTAG

Our aversion to making mistakes may be a result of the mindless learning of rules. Whether in art or life, we have to have a very clear idea of what the right thing is before we can do it the wrong way. When the weather report tells us that tomorrow is *likely* to be cloudy or that there's a 30 percent chance of rain, it is not a mistake if tomorrow turns out to be clear and sunny. In fact, science can only give us probabilities for its conclusions, although the reporting of science too often takes on an air of certainty unwarranted by the data from which it is derived. Taking conditional information and mindlessly imposing certainty on it leads to assuming any deviation from that certainty to be a mistake. Sometimes the outcome of this certainty can be tragic, as when we pump the brake pedal but shouldn't, and sometimes it can be merely humorous. In either case, it is ironic that we seek certainty in part to avoid mistakes, like skidding on ice, when it is this very certainty that may lead to the consequences we tried to avoid.

Interestingly, the lack of certainty can be an unexpected asset. Recently, my printer was malfunctioning. I don't really understand the nature of the conversation between my computer and printer, but I ultimately tried telling the computer that the printer was a different model than it in fact is. It worked. I have no idea why, but I'm reasonably sure that if I knew a bit more (but not everything) about computers and printers, the solution I found would not have seemed reasonable and I probably wouldn't have tried it. When we don't expect to know something completely, we don't see ourselves as making mistakes, we see ourselves as learners. Ironically, when we know something really well, we may be unaware of how much we don't really know about it. Rather than proceeding like investigators to learn more, we tend to limit our possibilities for mindful solutions.[4]

The literary critic John Gardner once wrote, "Most supposed aesthetic absolutes prove relative under pressure." Indeed, for any of the rules of good writing, notable exceptions can be found. If there is no rule, there can be no mistake. If the rule is to be followed absolutely, mistakes have been made, even by the best. The best, however, tend to use rules mindfully, that is, to guide rather than to govern. Consider a rule I learned long ago in school, that any expectations the author raises in a story need to be addressed and resolved by the end of the work. As Gardner reminds us, Shakespeare's Hamlet is known above all else for being indecisive. But how do we account for his decisive actions when he was exiled to England and the death that awaited him? Did Shakespeare simply not deal with the change in character so he could focus on the action between Hamlet and Claudius? Likewise, did Homer forget to tell us whether Achilles truly loved Briseis, or did the answer seem unimportant or obvious? Homer, like Shakespeare, raises expectations and then just abandons the reader, as he abandons a rule of good storytelling.

They are, of course, not alone. In one chapter of his novel *Absalom, Absalom!* William Faulkner describes a house as built out of wood, while a later chapter describes the same house as stone. The mistake doesn't detract from the novel. Instead, if anything, it reveals that there is a person behind the writing. As Gardner writes:

> *Art depends heavily on feeling, intuition, taste. It is feeling, not some rule, that tells the abstract painter to put his yellow here and there, not there, and may later tell him that it should have been brown, purple or pea-green. It's feeling that makes the composer break surprisingly from his key, feeling that gives the writer the rhythms of his sentences, the pattern of rise and fall in his episodes, the proportions of alternating elements, so that dialogue goes on only so long before a shift to description or narrative summary or some physical action.*

When we are mindful, we are cognizant of these feelings. When we fear mistakes and blindly follow rules, we remain cut off from them.

No course can tell us what details to choose for our experiments; no course can tell us what words to use to have an authentic interaction; no book can tell us what specific behavior will make us mindful in the moment. If I wrote a rule book for mindfulness and it were taken literally, clearly mindlessness would result. If you always put your right shoe on first but now put the left one on first, soon enough, that too will become mind-numbing.

No amount of study can tell us what content to choose, what colors to use, or how to compose a painting. In science as in art, no amount of study can tell us what details to include in an experiment. Each detail could be a mistake or lead to a new outcome. All of the many elements combine uniquely at each moment, and these combinations determine the next, and so on. Every choice affects every other one.

For some, such uncertainty represents an absence of personal control. From a mindful perspective, however, uncertainty creates the freedom to discover meaning. If there are meaningful choices, there is uncertainty. If there is no choice, there is no uncertainty and no opportunity for control. If we deem the number of choices so overwhelming that we refuse to engage them, there is no control. The theory of mindfulness insists that accepting uncertainty and the experience of personal control are inseparable.

Mistakes, Categories, and Perceptions

If you don't like something, change it. If you can't change it, change your attitude. Don't complain.
MAYA ANGELOU

When we evaluate other people's actions and results, we often see them as mistakes because we fail to recognize that their perspective was different from ours. It is not only the general population that may judge a different perspective as a mistake, some psychologists do as well. Consider the question, Which is more likely, spilling coffee or spilling hot coffee?

If they were to apply what is called the inclusion rule, most psychologists would presume the correct answer to be "coffee," since the category "coffee" includes all kinds of coffee, hot, cold, iced, et cetera. It seems quite clear that if you spill hot coffee, you are spilling coffee, and therefore the risk of spilling coffee is greater. The answer to the question, by this reasoning, is both straightforward and definitive. If we look more closely, however, we can understand how it may well not be.

Instead of seeing one category, "coffee," that is made up of various kinds of coffee (hot, warm, iced), one could create different categories, for example, hot and cold beverages. After all, when many of us want a cup of hot coffee but can't find one, we reach for hot tea or hot chocolate, but we do not reach for iced coffee. For some of us, hot chocolate has a lot more in common with other hot drinks than it does with a cold glass of chocolate milk. It is quite reasonable to suggest that hot coffee is not, for some, a category of coffee. It is its own category. It is the property "hot" that defines the larger category, not "coffee." Likewise, my experience might lead me to imagine that the category "coffee" contains only "hot coffee" if I've never tried iced coffee.

The question then amounts to which drink (category) am I more likely to spill, drink A or drink B? The names may be similar, but the drinks for me are as different as Coke and milk. The answer "hot coffee" is, in this light, completely sensible.

I asked this question of a friend who I did not think considered things like inclusion rules, and she answered, "Coffee." Intrigued, I then asked how she came to her answer. She replied that "if I want to drink hot coffee, I have to drink it right away because it gets cool quickly. On the other hand, if I don't want it hot, it can stay around all day, and then there are lots of chances for it to spill." It makes sense. Even though the answer "coffee" doesn't reveal it, she too was responding to "coffee" as a category different from "hot coffee" and not a subset of it.

Much of the time when we think that people are giving us a "wrong" answer, we should reconsider what their perspective might be and how it may lead them to frame the question. Perhaps, in the absence of asking them, we should ask ourselves, To what questions would the answer given be correct?

Categories and perspective are critical to the way we approach the world. Joan Miró felt that nudes constituted their own category of art. It is not hard to see why when we note the vast difference between his paintings and other artists' paintings of nudes. In some real sense, it seems strange even to think of them in the same category, leading us, perhaps, to a greater question: When years ago we were told we weren't talented at art, was it art like Miró's or some other paintings of nudes that our critics had in mind?

The Illusion of Predictability

Mistakes are almost always of a sacred nature. Never try to correct them. On the contrary: rationalize them, understand them thoroughly. After that, it will be possible for you to sublimate them.
SALVADOR DALÍ

Once during a lecture, the physicist Richard Feynman was asked a question about the use of data to verify an idea. To the surprise of his audience, his reply began with a discourse on license plates.

> *You know, the most amazing thing happened to me tonight. I was coming here, on the way to the lecture, and I came in through the parking lot. And you won't believe what happened. I saw a car with the license plate ARW 357. Can you imagine? Of all the millions of license plates in the state, what was the chance that I would see that particular one tonight? Amazing!*[5]

Feynman then went on to calculate the odds of having seen the license plate ARW 357, which he estimated as over 18 million to one. His point was that, going forward, everything is improbable; after the fact, we often make it seem that, of course, it occurred as it did. Before the fact the odds that we can predict the event are astronomical. All events, indeed, are improbable, so why do we think we can predict events in the future?

In fact, if we didn't believe in the illusion of predictability, we couldn't make mistakes. First, we need to believe that our actions will result in particular outcomes to conclude that we have failed in reaching them. And then we have to believe that if our actions don't result in the outcomes we've predicted, we ought to feel negatively. It would be odd, after all, if making a mistake resulted in a moment of celebration for us. Let's take these points up in turn.

Our extraordinary ability to make sense of our worlds when we *look back* at our actions makes it seem that we should have/could have known the consequences of our behavior going *forward* in time. Once we realize that all actions can have several meanings, it becomes clearer how difficult it is to predict subsequent actions. Take the simple act of John raising his right arm and accidentally making contact with Sam's shoulder. What will John do next? How will Sam respond? Before we can even begin to fool ourselves into knowing the answers, we have to interpret John's intentions and Sam's interpretation of John's intentions—which probably depends in part on how hard John struck him, which may depend on how strong John is, which could depend on whether his recent activities had left him more tired than usual, not to mention how well he slept last night, and so on. Of course, Sam might or might not consider all these factors in his response. Unlike with the appearance of license plates, it's hard to know where to begin the calculations. The unpredictability of even simple actions involving just two players becomes quite clear when we try to predict the future rather than justify events after the fact.

Jane, while carrying a glass of milk upstairs, passes the couch in the living room and hears a car pulling into her neighbor's garage. What happens next? There is, of course, no way of knowing. Even if we arbitrarily limit the question to what Jane does with the milk, it is still hard to know. Should we consider her prior experiences with milk? Over her lifetime she has heated it (sometimes making it warm, sometimes very hot), she has decided after a sip or two to add chocolate to it, sipped it, gulped it, spilled it, and even thrown it, let's say. Even if knowing her experience with milk felt convincing somehow, that was then and this is now. Jane has never been this age before, this mature, this strong, this carefree, and each of these aspects of who she is right now could affect each of the possibilities regarding what she might do with the glass of milk. Let's say Jane was startled by the car and spilled the milk. After the fact it's easy to believe that we should have seen it coming. She's very pleased about some news she just received and, lost in her thoughts, not paying adequate attention to what she's doing. She had tripped over a wastebasket at work earlier in the day and, once home, didn't even hear the phone ring. Clearly, she's in another world right now, and that's why the milk spilled. Actually, I miswrote. Jane took the glass of milk upstairs and sipped it slowly, enjoying it as if it were a fine wine.

Looking back, it is easy to create a causal chain of events that appears to be precise and unavoidable. The problem is that, especially if we are clever, we can make any event look as though it was predictable. In the 1960s, Jerome Bruner and Mary Potter conducted an important study that illustrated the problem with our tendency to make these predictions.[6] They asked participants to look through an apparatus at an unfocused image for either a short or a relatively long period of time before the image was brought into focus. Participants simply had to report what the stimulus was as soon as they recognized it. Those who were shown the unfocused image for a longer period took longer to identify it correctly even as the image became focused. Uncomfortable with the uncertainty, they made predictions— they guessed at what the image was—then tended to stick to those incorrect identifications even as the image became clearer.

Thinking that we should know something makes it hard for us not to know. But if we live our lives looking forward mindfully, the events before us are still to be categorized. We can't predict if we don't know what it is we are predicting.[7]

Understanding Predictions

Man will never reach the moon regardless of all future scientific advances.
DR. LEE DE FOREST, inventor of the vacuum tube, 1957

There is no likelihood man can ever tap the power of the atom.
ROBERT MILLIKAN, Nobel Prize in Physics, 1923

I think there is a world market for maybe five computers.
THOMAS WATSON, Chairman of IBM, 1943

There is no reason for any individual to have a computer in their home.
KENNETH OLSEN, President and Founder
of Digital Equipment Corporation, 1977

Airplanes are interesting toys but of no military value.
MARSHAL FERDINAND FOCH, French Military Strategist and
Future World War I Commander, 1911

Television won't be able to hold on to any market it captures after the first six months. People will soon get tired of staring at a plywood box every night.
DARRYL F. ZANUCK, Head of Twentieth Century-Fox, 1946

Predict today and lose tomorrow?
ELLEN J. LANGER

All of these predictions were made by very smart people who thought they could foresee the future. In fact, we all do this to a greater extent than we realize. Whether we decide to engage in an activity or not is often based on our implicit predictions about how well we'll perform. Therefore, in the interest of opening up our willingness to engage in creative pursuits, let's look more closely at what actually goes into making a prediction. Our illusion of predictability springs mostly from a tangle of poor assumptions that we make about ourselves and the world:

1. We tend to confuse prediction and post-diction. Knowing in advance that something will occur is very different from knowing that it did occur.

2. We enjoy a large degree of freedom in deciding whether our predictions are correct. The more abstract our level of analysis, the easier it is to be correct, and we are good at making our predictions abstract. For example, at any particular moment it is easier to predict that someone will "do something nice" than to predict what that nice thing will be. And so it becomes easy to imagine that we're good predictors when we aren't.

3. We don't keep in mind that predicting for the general case is very different from predicting any particular instance.

4. When we predict, we often mindlessly reduce the options to two alternatives, making it more possible to be correct. It is easier to predict, of course, that someday a woman will be president than to predict who the first woman president will be and when she'll be elected.

5. Our prediction that we are good predictors then leads us to a memory search of our successes, which are readily found. Unfortunately, so too would be our failures, if we chose to look for them. So while we are often correct, we would find that we are just as often incorrect if we stopped to notice.

6. The more we think about something, the more likely it seems, and the more predictable we feel it is. My research on the illusion of control shows that the more I think about my lottery ticket, for example, the more confident I'll become that I'll win.

7. We typically make predictions before we take action. The action taken may well become a self-fulfilling prophecy, falsely reinforcing our belief in our ability to predict. Imagine this time that I'm going to carry a full cup of coffee into the other room. Knowing how clumsy I can be, I imagine that I might spill it. The more I think about it, the more reasons I come up with that I might spill it, and the more certain I am about my prediction. As I head out of the room, my anxiety leads me to spill the coffee, confirming my ability to predict.

For all these reasons, the illusion of predictability is strong, while in reality we aren't very good predictors at all. But if we can't predict, then it may not make sense to think of unplanned outcomes as mistakes. Even if we could predict them, unplanned outcomes would deserve to be called "mistakes" only if we could say with assurance (that is, once again predict) that we will find them to be, in some way, "bad." Even in our reactions to outcomes, it turns out that we are bad predictors. We are often told that it will look better in the morning. When we experience a negative outcome, we deal with it and in so doing make it less negative than we thought it would be.

Researchers have shown how poor our predictions are when we engage in "affective forecasting," predicting how we'll feel in response to future events. Their studies have demonstrated that we frequently are wrong about how we are going to feel after we relocate to another city, break up with a romantic partner, learn we have a serious illness, or fail to secure a promotion. We tend to overemphasize how a negative outcome will affect us. In reality, people are much more resilient than they realize, and "bad outcomes" often are not nearly as bad as people thought they would be. In short, we can take more risks knowing that our "mistakes" (if that's even what they turn out to be) won't be as negative as we imagine they will be.

We predict so that we can control, yet predicting, ironically, decreases our control. Let's imagine I'm riding through the woods and I predict that low-hanging branches can lead to danger. I then become vigilant and notice if any branches are in the way. My prediction has made the presence of trees and branches very salient to me, but as I race through the woods, my horse stumbles on a boulder I didn't see. Our predictions make us vigilant with respect to particulars and in so doing blind us to what otherwise would be visible.

Suppose that most of my paintings have been fun, but someone comments that she prefers serious paintings to my dog paintings. What would happen if I took this to mean (if I predicted) that serious paintings would win more approval from others? First, I've mindlessly accepted the notion that serious and fun are mutually exclusive categories. Second, I'm mindlessly letting the prediction dictate the content of the next painting, rather than painting what at the moment feels most appropriate. If I don't feel serious and I paint a serious painting, is it likely to be as good as one that comes from a more authentic feeling? The prediction decreases my choices. Without the prediction, I might paint a humorous painting, a serious painting, a humorous painting that reveals serious content, or a painting whose seriousness serves the purpose of poking fun at itself.

If we ask people how often they expect to be successful at

something they know well, a common answer is around 90 percent of the time. Have you ever heard anyone say he feels that he was simply in the 10 percent part of life after making a mistake? I haven't. Instead, too often the mistake leads him to feel incompetent. Even if we acknowledge that, at least in theory, we know we will make mistakes, we often become all too annoyed at ourselves when we do. I play a lot of doubles tennis, and I tend to play with others at my level of skill. On each point, one of the four players will necessarily miss or fail to reach a shot. Still, whoever misses seems to feel bad.

Once we realize that we can control our psychological experience of events, negative outcomes all but disappear. In fact, a better way to view mistakes is to see them as cues for learning, puzzles to solve. When a computer glitch occurs, it can become a detective story, resulting in great excitement once it is solved. When a tennis shot is hit long, it can become a matter of figuring out why, making us better players on the next shot.

What would it mean to not make mistakes? We cannot know exactly how things will be, even if we've done them before. Sometimes we'll go a little too far, or do a little too much, and sometimes not enough. And there is always a way for someone to find fault, even if we do it just as we thought we should. There is a humorous, albeit apocryphal, joke Freudian therapists tell that speaks volumes here. "The patient who comes early is displaying *anxiety,* he who comes late is offering *resistance.* But if he regularly comes on time, he is *compulsive.*"

To not make a mistake we have to err on the side of caution and not try anything new. Such a life would be deadening, literally and figuratively. What's more, we limit ourselves if we play it too safe. If I enter debates about psychology only with freshmen or play tennis only with beginners, I narrow my experience considerably. In fact, if I put myself in situations only where I can guarantee no mistakes, I am also guaranteeing no learning and no passion. A hole in one on every hole; a home run on every at bat; an ace on every serve, all sound great unless we actually imagine how boring the games would become for us. Mistakes symbolize our willingness to be in the present. Mistakes show us what else we might learn.

The Perfection of Mistakes

Artists who seek perfection in everything are those who cannot find it in anything.
EUGÈNE DELACROIX

There is an old Chinese proverb that says, if an idea is present, the brush may be spared performance. My friend Bill was an avid collector of African art. We've often discussed how many of his most compelling pieces are incomplete—a leg missing from a piece of sculpture, for example. Why might this be? To me, the more complete and perfect the work, the less there is for the mind to work with. Incompleteness and imperfection are engaging.

All too often we seek perfection, only to find it leads us to mindlessness. When we were very young, turning on a light was an accomplishment. Once we mastered it, we tended to turn on the light mindlessly. Oddly, we find ourselves in the position of performing tasks either perfectly mindlessly or imperfectly mindfully.

Painting by numbers, literally and figuratively, where there is a rigid expectation that things will be a certain way, is not likely to advance the individual or the culture. On the level of the particular, the world is always changing, despite our attempts to hold it still. We imagine we do so successfully because we confuse the stability of our mind-sets with the stability of the underlying phenomenon. In painting and in life, if we know exactly what we want to do and how to do it, without availing ourselves of whatever may be new in the current situation, the result is typically mindless behavior. If we are not going to show up for our own performance, why bother doing it at all? If we know just where we want to go from the outset, and try to confirm all our expectations, what is the reward for our effort?

If we are mindfully creative, the circumstances of the moment will tell us what to do. Robert Frost makes the point about writing poetry: "It should be the pleasure of the poem itself to tell how it can. It assumes direction with the first line laid down. It is but a trick poem and no poem at all if the best of it was thought of first and saved for the last. It finds its own name as it goes and discovers the best waiting for it in some final phrase. No surprise for the writer, no surprise for the reader."[8]

We all repeat expressions such as "It's only human to make a mistake," with the understanding that mistakes are to be avoided. Yes, it *is* human to make mistakes, but that is often one of the best aspects of being human. We can approach our world imperfectly and mindfully or perfectly and mindlessly. When we know it so well that it becomes second nature, we are doing so mindlessly. If we approach it mindfully, we are allowing ourselves to make mistakes.

Painting taught me not just to be tolerant of myself when I make mistakes but actually to welcome them. Mistakes provide the opportunity to be mindful. When, by choice or by necessity, we find ourselves in the present, the details of the present can tell us what to do.

5

The Rule of Absolutes

I have eaten
the plums
that were in
the icebox
and which
you were probably
saving
for breakfast

Forgive me
they were delicious
so sweet
and so cold.

WILLIAM CARLOS WILLIAMS

WHAT A WONDERFUL POEM. OR, AS SOME HAVE WONDERED, IS IT just a note Williams left on the refrigerator?[1] To invest the mundane with meaning and beauty, and in so doing to make the world personal, is to live a personal renaissance. It's when we imagine that the world is apart from us that we are led astray. For many people, it's the fear that their creative endeavors won't live up to some external standard that keeps them from living a more creative life. But surely if we create something, it can and should have special meaning for us. And if critics are willing to find art in giant hamburgers, soup cans, and toilets, why shouldn't we find meaning in our own doodles and master-pieces?

What is Art, and are there standards that we must reach or rules we must follow for our creative efforts to be meaningful? Most of us think that there are, and when we set out to try something new, we first look carefully at the work of others that has received high praise. We watch others creating Art in the be-lief that we can discern the right way to do it ourselves. We im-plicitly assume there is an inherent logic to doing whatever we don't know how to do, whether it is Art, a sport, or a new task at work. The problem with this approach is that we usually end up on the sidelines watching, rather than engaging the activity and taking control of it. We are too readily guided by the expe-rience and opinions of others, no matter whether they apply to us or our situation.

Our world has been fashioned largely by people. People cre-ate the products we use, make the laws we follow, write the books we study in high school. Despite all of our efforts to per-fect ourselves, the truth is that people have limited knowledge, mixed motivations, biases, and any number of other limita-tions. Many of us know this conceptually, even if we don't think very often about how it affects our approach to the world. And so we experience our world, more often than not, as if it exists independent of human involvement. We take the things we use, the rules we follow, and the information we rely on as if they are true in some absolute sense, regardless of context or perspec-tive. We have become oblivious to the part others play and have played in deciding much of what we take for granted. This is unfortunate, for by doing so, we give up new choices and lose the opportunity to take more control of our lives.

By creating an external world, then treating it as if it is independent of ourselves, we rob ourselves of our individuality and the opportunity to meet our needs. We can regain control, but only when we put people and context back into the equation. Compare a sign that warns you to "keep off the grass" with one that reads, "Ellen says keep off the grass." The first demands obedience without hesitation, whereas the second invites us to ask, "Who is Ellen and why does she want me to keep off the grass? Who does she think she is?" Too often, we follow rules as if they have an inherent logic that is reasonable across all contexts. We are taught to think inside the box. Then we are taught to think outside the box. What I want us to ask is, Who put the box there?

Putting People Back into the Equation

The defining function of the artist is to cherish consciousness.
MAX EASTMAN

Many years ago I went to an Amish dinner that was open to the public and attracted a large crowd of non-Amish diners. We all sat at long wooden tables, family style, and the benches grew rather uncomfortable as the evening went on. A good while after dessert had been served and eaten, we remained fidgeting in our seats, waiting to be told what to do next. Nobody knew if it was acceptable to leave because there was no recognizable cue that signaled when an "Amish" dinner was over. Finally, not able to sit still any longer, I got up. Immediately, everyone else followed. Obviously, the others had been as uncomfortable sitting there as I had been, so why didn't they leave until I did?

The fear of violating a rule encourages us to look to others to find out what to do. To follow others is fine, unless to do so is to our disadvantage. But would we always mindlessly follow a rule if we knew who created it and why they did so? If not, then it is important to put a face to the things we implicitly treat as objective truths, to make certain that they make sense in the current context.

Recently when I was playing tennis my opponents began arguing over whether "the rules" stated that they should move in concert to play the net and the backcourt or whether one should cover the net and the other play back. As the discussion grew more heated, I wondered whose rules they were trying to follow. Never being able to resist offering wanted or unwanted help, I asked a few questions. "Doesn't who you're playing against make a difference, at least for intermediate players like ourselves?" "If your opponent has a great drop shot, do you both want to play back?" "If your opponent has a great lob, do you both want to play the net? Or if your opponents have neither, do you want to pass up the opportunity to intimidate them by coming to the net together?" It didn't make sense to me that there could be a rule that could apply to all possible situations in a sport as subtle as tennis. To my mind, my friends had become governed by their sense of the rules instead of their sense of the situation in which they were playing.

Our transition from being rule-governed to being rule-guided naturally flows from the moment we start asking ourselves when was the rule made, by whom, and with what information and motivation. We tend to learn one set of rules and then follow them forever, never asking ourselves these questions. It wouldn't be so bad if we continued learning rules, and in the process discovered that some of the new ones conflict with the old. That would put us back into the game of asking questions about the rules. More typically, however, we stop learning any new rules once we have found "the" way.[2]

Finding the Context of Rules

There are no rules for good photographs, there are only good photographs.
ANSEL ADAMS

In one of Vincent van Gogh's letters to his brother Theo, he complains that he can't seem to use color properly, an assertion that appears ridiculous to us today. No matter how proficient we are at what we do, most of us are able to find a way to draw comparisons with some ideal or existing yardstick that keeps us from recognizing the value of what we are doing. That's unfortunate, because rules are, by their very nature, mindless limitations on our attention to the context in which we do things. But this need not be the case.

We can see past the limitations that rules present. One simple way is to remember to ask ourselves, "Who says so? Who decided on this rule, and how did they come to the decision?" Even, for example, such hard-and-fast rules as "drive on the right side of the road" can reasonably be examined. How was the rule derived? What surface did its creators have in mind? Imagine there is an ice patch on the right side of the road and there are no other cars on the road. It would seem that steering to the left would be more sensible than adhering to the rule. We are better off in understanding the uncertainty that existed when the rules were created. Yes, at least in the United States we probably should drive on the right-hand side of the road generally, but remembering that sometimes it would be safer to move to the left lane can make us more aware of the moment, for it is in the moment that we have to decide whether or not to break the rule.

Once, while consulting at a nursing home, I happened to be in the director's office when a nurse walked in complaining about one of the residents. Apparently she didn't want to have dinner in the dining room, as policy dictated, preferring instead to eat a peanut butter sandwich in her room. I asked what was wrong with that, to which the director replied, "What if everyone wanted to do that?" Well, if everyone wants to do it, I thought, perhaps it ought to be done. If everyone ate peanut butter sandwiches, the home would save a lot of money on food. Or, I supposed, it might mean the food in the dining room needed improving. If everyone wants to "break" the rule, perhaps it should be broken. And if only a few people don't follow the rule, there seems to me to be little harm typically being done. But the nurse was treating the offender as though she were violating some moral imperative because of her presumption that the rule made sense to all people and across all contexts. Recognizing that this is rarely, if ever, true can free us from mindlessly following rules when they are not in our best interest.

Let me be clear. I am not advocating mindless rule breaking or a lack of respect for rules that our culture has generated over the course of time. I am, instead, suggesting that we let rules and routines guide our behavior but question them as we find ourselves in new and different contexts. This is particularly important in our creative lives, where the rules often lead us to imagine we don't stand a chance at success. If the rules tell us that we have to gain a full understanding of fiction before we can write it well, many of us will never pick up a pen. But if we imagine that our context is different, that the rules don't need to apply to us, many of our inhibitions about creative engagement may fall to the wayside.

One Size Never Fits All

The minute one utters a certainty, the opposite comes to mind.
MAY SARTON

We should ask questions not just about rules but in all cases where others think something should fit into our lives but it doesn't. Given how different we are from one another, it is absurd to expect that one size fits all. Even when we are presented with choices, it is useful to remember that someone decided what those choices should be. When buying clothes, we all understand that sizes vary from label to label, and often a size ten in one case is the perfect fit and in another it's a size twelve. Standards are everywhere in our lives. The shelves in the kitchen are a prescribed height, toilets a standard size, car seats adjust only front to back.

If we take each of these instances and ask who came up with the choice, based on what criteria, the larger argument becomes clearer. I reach for a dish on the top shelf and drop it. Am I clumsy or simply shorter than the person for whom the shelf was originally designed? Someone very tall can be quite uncomfortable in a conventional bathroom. Who chose the size of the toilet seat or its height from the floor? If we asked such questions more often, we might find a reason to customize fixtures or create ones that have more choices built in. Most car seats move to accommodate different leg lengths, but they could just as easily be designed to turn to allow someone "disabled" to enter more easily. Indeed, people often become more disabled by the design than by any limitations they may have.

We all become disabled when we don't fit the assumptions that went into the design. Not that long ago standard dosages for medications were set using the twenty-something, mostly male medical student as the norm. As a result, elderly adults, whose bodies typically retain medications longer, were often overmedicated. If older adults had been the norm for dosage testing, twenty-something adult males would have been undermedicated, but neither needs to be the case.

Science, which prides itself on its objectivity, usually hides its choices from us even as it reports its findings. Many design choices that go into even our most rigorous scientific studies affect their outcomes. Greater awareness of these choices would make the findings less absolute and more useful to us. In fact, scientific research is reported in journals as probability statements, although textbooks and popular magazines often report the same results as absolute facts. This change is done to make the science easier for nonscientists to understand. But what it does, instead, is deceive us by promoting an illusion of stability. That illusion is fostered by taking people out of the equation—what choices the researcher made in setting up the experiment, on whom was it tested, and under what circumstances.

We need to learn to ask for whom the "absolute" was designed and with what goals in mind. Were we to do so, we would be able to find ways of making the "absolute" fit our own circumstances better. In those situations where our circumstances don't match the group in mind, it is all the more important that we know this.

Finding Reasons for What We Do

No amount of skillful invention can replace the essential element of imagination.
EDWARD HOPPER

In my seminars I often give my students the route of one of Boston's annual parades and ask them to explain why it was chosen. They easily generate a number of quite plausible reasons, like concern for safety, maximum viewing potential, or preservation of traffic flow. When they've finished, I explain to them that the parade's founder, who happens to be a friend of mine, planned the route thirty years ago because, on the day of the first parade, she had to be at the starting location at the time the parade was scheduled to begin and she wanted to end up at her friend's house when it was over.

We all are wonderful at finding reasons for what we do, even if, as the psychologist Robert Abelson says, we are not very good at doing what we find reasons for. Typically, we take mundane actions and justify them in larger terms, offering moral explanations for our behavior which make it appear that we could have or should have acted no other way. Suppose that, not long after September 11, I decide to go shopping because I felt I "needed" shoes and ask a friend to come along. My friend doesn't want to go and calls my behavior frivolous, especially in a time of national crisis. I might counter that shopping is important for the economy and thus I am being patriotic. The problem with calling upon these grander explanations for our choices is that it can lead us to be foolishly judgmental. It is fine if I want to go shopping and my friend doesn't. It is not fine for someone to be frivolous, nor is it fine to be unpatriotic. These are not, however, fair assessments of either of our motivations.

In general, we live our lives in the details, fully aware that the details are subject to change. In a quest for stability, we tend to look for general explanations for why things are. Again, we confuse the stability of our mind-sets with the stability of the underlying phenomenon by not attending to the ever-changing details. We seek this stability to feel in control, but it is this mistaken presumption of stability that robs us of control.

In this way, we create an external world and then forget that people like us did the creating and could have just as readily made different choices. We then operate in this world without having it speak back to us. We make choices all the time, some important, some trivial. But even the trivial choices can be quite instructive. Suppose you have four mugs on the shelf but usually select one for your morning coffee. Why did you choose the one you did? What does that choice tell you? By picking the same mug every day, you create an absolute and shut off a series of choices you in fact have, keeping the world fixed. Imagine how you might otherwise enjoy your coffee if you chose anew each time. Imagine further that you asked yourself why you made the particular selection you did.

The answers to these questions are not always readily available to us, but when they are, they allow the external world we've created to serve as a window into our internal lives. On occasion I like eating yogurt with a very small spoon, and I would miss something about the experience if a small spoon were not available to me. But why do I have this preference at this time and not others? Sometimes a spoon is just a spoon. Sometimes it is not. We all pay attention to life's big decisions, but there really aren't that many of them. Life's actually made up of lots of smaller choices that we could be making but mindlessly don't, choices that could reveal much about ourselves.

Absolutes and Creativity

If you approach an opera as though it were something
that always went a certain way, that's what you get.
I approach an opera as though I didn't know it.
SARAH CALDWELL

The canvas, the written piece, or the song selected for our instrument can serve as a mirror for us. But they won't if we approach the world as if it were something external to us rather than a function of individual or group or society's choices. Indeed, in our creative lives we constantly search for absolutes that we can make use of, despite the fact that these absolutes limit us far more than they help us.

Consider artistic movements, which, like fashion, change over time. What is in today is out tomorrow. Yet we still fear and follow the absolutes of the day without recognizing that the rules will change. Recently a friend was going to a wedding and asked me, panicked, about what to wear. I replied with two simple questions: Who decided what is appropriate? Will anyone stop being your friend if you wear the "wrong" thing? I told her that if she really cared about fashion, she'd know what to wear. If she really didn't care about fashion, why care now?

As already noted, Édouard Manet's paintings that defined the advent of Impressionism were at first harshly criticized by the art critics whose acceptance he thought critical to his success. Today, paintings such as *Le Déjeuner sur l'herbe* are widely admired and considered benchmarks in the history of art. Are we to think that they were inherently bad when he submitted them for exhibition, only to become inherently good at some later date? Of course not. By observing how likes and dislikes change over time, we become freer to pursue our own desires. By learning to ask who made the rule and when and why, we will come to this freedom more easily.

The fun of creating is to create, not to follow a list of rules. Mastery in all things, I believe, may come from an implicit understanding that rules were made by people under particular circumstances. When the circumstances change, the rule should be modified. How do we know how to do so? We know how to modify rules when we are being authentic. When we are authentic, we draw on our idiosyncratic experience. This experience tells us what details to include, what details to exclude, and how to describe them. We make our choices based on what is important to us at the time. No rules can do that.

Itiel Dror and I have conducted studies that show clearly the readiness with which we accept absolutes and the limits they impose on us in our creative endeavors.[3] The task we set for the participants, undergraduate students, was to build a bridge over an imaginary river using small wooden blocks. Half the participants were first shown models of bridges—some one model, some two—constructed from the blocks, the other half weren't shown any models. In our first study, 92 percent of the group that saw the examples built bridges identical to the ones they had been shown, while only 8 percent of the other group used such formations.

We then asked participants to build a bridge that was as tall as they could make it, and we measured the variety of solutions each group developed. Strongly influenced by the model they had just seen, the one-model group found an easy solution. They constructed their bridges exactly like the model they had been shown. The example suggested to participants that this model was that right way to solve the problem, and they did not think to build their bridge in other ways. But the group shown two models and the group not shown any models outper- formed the single-model group in that they consistently devel- oped more solutions to the problem. Those who didn't have any model to work from came up with the most types of bridges, and those shown two models, while less prolific in the variety of solutions they presented, demonstrated that being given two examples suggested there were choices to be made.

We see a great variety in the world around us, but we don't imagine having many choices available to us. We tend to pre- sume that there *is* a best choice and become paralyzed because we do not know what it is. If we make the wrong choice, we will seem stupid. Most people don't realize that the walls in our houses were painted white because the builders thought it would be easier to sell houses with white walls. After all, if a dining room wall were painted a deep purple that didn't suit a particular buyer, the sale might be lost. The goal for the builders who have chosen the color of many walls in our houses, then, is purposely to avoid any hint of individuality. Knowing this, we may find it easier to create something more to our own liking when it comes time to repaint the dining room. Painting walls, just like painting canvases, can be an opportunity to be creative.

When we put people back in the equation, we are able to make different attributions for our choices and our behavior; we are, in essence, free to become more creative. My student Adam Grant recently joined me in an experimental test of this idea.[4] We divided the participants, more than sixty Harvard undergraduates, into two groups, giving both of them a simple enough task—to create a drawing—suggesting to half of them that they draw a horse. We then divided our subjects into three groups, further testing the impact of perceived choice. One group was first shown a single painting of a horse and were told it was created by a famous artist. The second group was shown nine very different horses painted by well-known artists from several cultures and periods, suggesting that there isn't just one way to represent a horse. A third group, our control, wasn't shown any artworks. All the participants, when finished, were asked to evaluate their drawings. We then asked other people, who hadn't been participants, to rank the drawings.

The results confirmed our hypothesis: perceived choice and enhanced subjectivity led to increased artistic creativity as rated by blind volunteers. Seeing the different ways a horse could be represented suggested that artists are able to make choices, that there isn't any single way to draw a horse successfully. By implicitly recognizing that people were able to make their own decisions about what to draw, rather than having to conform to an absolute, ideal horse, participants were freed to make choices for themselves. As we predicted, those participants who drew a horse after seeing the nine different horses were the most successful. Both they and the people we brought in to judge the results liked their drawings more than the drawings of the other two groups.

But art is, of course, subjective by its very nature. Could we affect some more general, purportedly more objective, aspects of our lives by putting people back in the equation? We considered that our society is replete with tests to measure "objectively" a host of skills and abilities. In addition to tests of abilities, such as the SAT, ACT, MCAT, LSAT, and GRE tests, we have several tests of intelligence. These tests have all been standardized and made as objective as the test makers could think to do. In fact, because of the widespread belief in their objectivity, those who perform poorly on these tests are more limited in their options for further education, may spend a lifetime in self-recrimination, and often avoid entering careers or taking up activities for which they believe they have no ability because of their performance on the tests.

While any particular test may accurately predict success, that does not mean that some other test would not have been an even better predictor. One could perform poorly on one of these tests but score well on another. For instance, the psychologist Martin Seligman found that the Attributional Style Questionnaire—a scale measuring optimism—is a more reliable predictor of academic success in college than the ACT.[5] The negative effects of these tests for those who do poorly on them have been discussed at length by others; let's consider here how we can avoid any negative consequences if we must take these tests. The way, essentially, is to offset their presumed objectivity by putting people back in the equation.

In another study, Adam Grant and I asked participants to take an exam, purportedly on reasoning skills.[6] One group, which we called the "objective group," read introductory materials that explained:

> *We are attempting to compare the reasoning skills of undergraduates at various schools in the Boston area, by asking them to complete the following ten question test. This test is called the Reasoning Skills Inventory, and it was developed by the Miller Foundation.*

The other, "subjective" group were given a different introduction:

> *We are attempting to compare the reasoning skills of undergraduates at various schools in the Boston area, by asking them to complete the following ten question test. These questions are taken from the Reasoning Skills Inventory, which was developed by eight people working at the Miller Foundation. The test that these eight people developed has 200 questions. We are asking you to complete 10 questions taken from the 200 question test.*

In this way, we made clear to the second group that the test was created by people and explained that the questions were chosen from many possible questions. This is the context of the standardized tests we take. They are written by people who are fallible, and the questions represent only a small subset of all the questions that might be on the tests. The fact that most people are oblivious to this very real context allows a subjective test to appear objective.

We asked the participants to wait while we scored their tests, informing them that we would return in a few minutes with their results. Without any regard to their actual performance, we reported to half of each group that they had scored very well and to the other half that they had scored poorly. For those who scored well, there was no difference in whether their scores led them to believe the test was objective or subjective. This was not the case, however, for those who were told they had scored poorly. Those who had been cued that the test had been made up by people choosing questions from a large pool of potential questions were protected from feeling incompetent. They saw the test not as an absolute indicator of their skill but rather as a possible indicator, context-dependent and subject to change. After all of the participants received their feedback, we asked the subjects to help move some boxes from the next room, acknowledging that we would understand if they didn't have time to do this. Those participants in the "objective" condition were less likely to help. Putting people back into the equation resulted in both higher self-esteem and a greater willingness to be there for another person.

Next, we assessed the generality of our hypothesis. We created scenarios that simply asked people what they would do in situations that either were stated objectively or had their person-nature revealed. For example, people in one group were told to imagine they are in the hospital, have just used a bedpan, and are very uncomfortable. They see the nurse outside their door, engaged in some activity, versus seeing nurse Betty Johnson outside, busy with some activity. How likely are they to interrupt her? We used scenarios that were personal, impersonal, and interpersonal, and across all of them participants were willing to exercise more control once we put the people back into the equation.

Putting people back in the equation reintroduces the uncertainty that was masked by their absence and can lead to positive effects. The studies just discussed suggest that we allow our- selves to be more creative when we do not mindlessly follow ab- solutes and that, if we perform well, we are more likely to be easier on ourselves and make external attributions for our fail- ures. Unveiling the mask of certainty is also likely to increase our information search—now we have reason to pay attention; we experience a decrease in the stress that often results from the fear of making the wrong decision; we increase our risk taking and try things we'd like to do but previously feared we'd do wrong; and, possibly most appealing, once we are aware of the inherent uncertainty in virtually all the situations in which we find ourselves, we should experience an increase in the number and kinds of exciting choices available to us.

The Nature of Absolutes

A primitive artist is an amateur whose work sells.
GRANDMA MOSES

Why do we create rules and absolutes if we tend to apply them mindlessly to our own detriment? What is their purpose if they only limit us? My theory is that the perception that we live in a world of limited resources leads us to create a system of hierar- chies and criteria for inclusion in order to establish a way to al- locate those resources. The limited numbers of places in Ivy League schools or on museum walls lead to the attitude that only a few people are intelligent enough to go to an Ivy League school or that there are only a few real artists whose work is worth showing. The criteria, good scores on SAT tests or the praise of critics, mean that only a few people are granted access. Now there isn't any real problem with allocating goods in this way, given the practical considerations, except that over time we tend to lose sight of the fact that the criteria for inclusion are arbitrary by definition and forget that, in a different context, different criteria may well be better determinants. As a result, we eventually grant these hierarchies and their criteria an ontological status.

The problems begin when some who are excluded from the group entitled to these resources take their exclusion to have psychological significance, rather than to be the result of convenience for a group of decision makers. Even if more resources become available, we tend to stick to the original criteria as if they had some sense separate from that with which decision makers invested them to justify the decision.

For example, because there are limited places in college classrooms, we need to find a way to exclude some potential students. We create a test, say the SAT, and overlook meaningful alternative criteria for selection. We take things a step further and overlook the alternative criteria for the kinds of questions that could be on the test. We then use scores to exclude. We can justify use of the scores by studies showing that they predict college performance and ignore the possibility that other tests inquiring into other abilities might do just as well.

If Harvard randomly selected students from those who applied, educated them, and granted them a Harvard degree, they might well be as successful as those who get in via their SAT scores. But if we allowed everyone to go to Harvard who wanted to, many would not want to go because the glamour of being "selected" would be gone.

In this way, the relationship between evaluation and the perception of limited resources is reciprocal and interactive, each causing the other. The consequence of these evaluations for all but perhaps the top 5 percent of applicants is a lifetime of feeling inadequate. People at ages fifty and sixty still degrade themselves based on how they performed on a test they took in their teens. Those who did not score high on tests like these should look at them once again as adults and consider the questions they could not answer. Do we really care if we don't know which picture represents the result of unfolding a piece of paper? Would we respect someone simply because she knows the answer to this or some other arbitrary question? As adults, shouldn't we realize that a group of people decided to ask this question, but that they could have asked a different one to which we might have known the answer? If we had these people in front of us so that we could judge them, the way they have indirectly judged us, what would we find? Couldn't we think of questions that they would not be able to answer? As long as we're oblivious to context, we don't think of things like this.

The psychologists Lee Ross, Teresa Amabile, and Julia Steinmetz conducted an interesting study in the 1970s that I've used as the basis for one of my favorite classroom demonstrations.[7] Sticking pretty close to the original study, I create an impromptu quiz show, choosing one student to pose questions to those who have volunteered to participate as contestants. I tell the student moderator that she is to make up all the questions for the quiz, *the only rule being that she know the answer to each question she asks.* It's quite a lot of fun to watch as the moderator tries to stump the eager contestants, which she always is able to do. When all the questions have been asked and answered, I ask the class to fill out a questionnaire that rates the intelligence of the participants. The results are surprising to the class. Even though they are perfectly aware that we all are able to devise questions others aren't likely to know the answers to—indeed, that the format of the game necessitates the moderator will always know the answer and the contestants may not—the moderator is always rated as more intelligent than the other participants.

In hindsight, it's easy to see that the unique interests and knowledge of the moderator allow her to ask questions the other students cannot answer. She might be quite knowledgeable about American artists and ask rather difficult questions about American Folk Art simply because she is taking a class on the subject. If the class knew that fact, would they have decided that she was more intelligent? Or would they simply have judged that the people who know more about American art know more about American art? Consider all the variations even a single question could have taken. She might have asked who Anna Mary Robertson was and stumped the contestants, or she might have asked who Grandma Moses (Anna Mary Robertson's more familiar name) was and received the correct answer. If we consider all the decisions that go into any test construction, then realize all the ways it could have been different, we might not evaluate ourselves so harshly when we do poorly on someone else's test. We don't typically realize, however, that it is someone else's test. Rather, the people disappear to help the test gain its status as an objective measure. How free we would be if we put people back in the equation.[8]

But Is It Art?

The first and last important rule for the creative writer, then, is that though there may be rules (formulas) for ordinary, easily publishable fiction—imitation fiction—there are no rules for real fiction, any more than there are rules for serious visual art or musical composition.
JOHN GARDNER

The philosopher George Dickie has argued that "Art" is whatever the art world takes to be Art.[9] Is our definition of Art really so dynamic and inclusive? I think that pragmatic concerns tend to govern us in insidious ways. If there is limited space in muse-

ums and galleries, limits are necessarily put on what we call Art
at any point in history. But when we build a new museum, the
prevailing criteria still tend to hold. Similarly, what we consider
a disease is in part determined by insurance companies, based
on their ability to fund treatment. If our symptoms are not part
of their definition, we may suffer more than just the absence of
reimbursement. We may question whether the symptoms are
real, as many did who suffered from chronic fatigue syndrome
before it was legitimized.

When space opens up in a museum or critics look for something new in the art world, Marcel Duchamp can buy a snow
shovel, title it *In Advance of the Broken Arm,* and it is deemed Art.
We too are able to engage the world around us mindfully. We
can look for and find aesthetic value in almost anything, and we
can appreciate it as Art. We need not be limited by the opinions
of "experts," who in turn are limited by what they perceive to be
limited resources.

We are often oblivious to the choices available even when we
know that a person is responsible, if that person is an expert.
No one would argue that the titles that accompany paintings
are subjectively derived. Nevertheless, the title is supplied by a
single other. This person, the artist in most cases, has a particular perspective that was derived in a particular historical context. The context in which we are viewing the painting may be
vastly different. If we created our own titles for some works,
those works might take on greater meaning for us. Yet we rarely
create from another's creations. That is, we take a work as is, as
if it could or should be no other way; in other words, as if there
is some objective way that makes the original choice valid.

In a recent experiment, Wendy Smith and I asked participants
to study a painting by Monet, giving it either a mysterious-
sounding title, its actual title, or no title but asking that partici-

pants make up a personally meaningful title.[10] We then timed how long they viewed the painting, and when they were finished, gave them a questionnaire that measured how much they liked the painting. Those who were asked to make up their own title both studied the painting the longest and reported that they liked it the most. By being asked to make up their own title, they were led to engage the painting all the more. It is interesting to me that we can always supply our own titles to the paintings we experience in museums and galleries, although it doesn't typically occur to us to do so. Perhaps we should, since it seems to add to our viewing experience. If we can learn that we can make things interesting for ourselves despite other people's criteria for excellence, we open up a whole world to ourselves. Not the least of all of this is that we may learn to look at our own work in this making-it-meaningful way.

If we see it as Art, it is Art. Willem de Kooning once gave Robert Rauschenberg a drawing that Rauschenberg erased. Then he exhibited the blank canvas under the title *Erased de Kooning Drawing, 1953*. So it is for our own works. If we take the time to make it meaningful, we have created a work of Art. *De gustibus non est disputandum* (matters of taste cannot be disputed).

Putting people back in the equation by asking, "Who said so, and who are they anyway?" frees us to individualize our experience, and we need to learn to ask this question of ourselves. When we look at our own creative work, something we have painted or written, for example, and decide it is not very good, what criteria are we using to make the evaluation? How did we choose them?

And who are we anyway?

6

The Mindlessness of Social Comparison

If you never assume importance
You never lose it.
LAO-TZU

Two rabbis are praying in the temple they've attended for thirty years.
They are scowling about how insignificant they are before the infinite
grandeur of the Creator. They listen to one another crying, "I am
nothing. I am nobody before you. I am a measly speck of filth—muck
on the windshield of your glorious Winnebago of Light." Then, a third
Jew walks in who the rabbis don't recognize. He sits himself next
to them and himself cries out in supplication: "I am nothing . . . nobody
before you . . ." The first rabbi looks to the second, frowns, and says:
"Who the heck is this guy, coming in here and thinking he's a nobody!?"
ANONYMOUS

DURING THE FALL ARTS FESTIVAL IN PROVINCETOWN, MANY ARTISTS open their studios to the public, and one October I thought it would be fun to add my name to the list of those participating. Copies of the artists' paintings and some information about them are made available at the office of the Chamber of Commerce, so people can see which studios they might like to visit. I liked the fact that any visitors who thought of coming to my studio could learn once there that I was a new artist and preview my work, meaning I could worry less about their being disappointed in what they would find.

One of the people who did come was a man about forty-five years old who had himself just started to paint. (At that time, I had been painting for about three years.) He asked many questions, which I answered as encouragingly as I could. He was clearly worried and uncertain about many things regarding his art, and as we spoke, I noticed the authority with which he was imbuing my remarks. Uncomfortable with his deeming me an "expert," I decided I should remind him that I too was new to painting. To my surprise, he simply glanced at the many paintings I had placed around the room and replied, "Well, that's easy for you to say, but I have only seven canvases."

Why did he feel compelled to compete with me, someone he had never heard of before that day and would probably never see again? Looking to better understand his response, I asked him what his purpose was in painting. Was he interested in making a living as an artist? He said he wasn't, he just wanted to have fun. Then what difference did it make, I asked, how much, or even how well or poorly, either he or I painted, or how many paintings either of us had done?

Many psychologists have studied social comparison and its effects on people. Comparing ourselves with other people can spur us on or it can be demoralizing. In one study of the comparisons we make with those we admire, Penelope Lockwood and Ziva Kunda found that when the accomplishments of others seem attainable, they will inspire us; when they seem unattainable, they may be undermining.[1] This finding raises a reasonable question: What determines our perception of how attainable the final outcome is? It depends on how we talk to ourselves about the others' behavior. If we attribute their success to their efforts, we are more likely to think that if we put in the effort we can achieve the result. If we attribute their success to talent we are lacking, we become demoralized. The artist who visited my house that day seemed to me to have arrived directly from that study.

A good deal of the work in psychology that deals with the self takes as a given that people will make evaluations, and from that assumption proceeds to examine the information people use and how they use it in making those evaluations. These theories work well enough. When people make evaluations, they do so in the manner suggested by these researchers. Their approach does not question, however, whether people need to be evaluative. I would argue that we can give up making these mindless evaluations, which only make it more difficult to begin any new creative endeavor.

The Social Comparison Sweepstakes

It has bothered me all my life that I do not paint like everybody else.
HENRI MATISSE

The most frequent evaluation people make is to compare themselves with other people. Comparison is certainly quite natural in our creative lives, for example, as those learning to play an instrument watch others who are slightly better players. Drawing such comparisons can be an effective way to learn, as long as we are aware of what we are doing. But too often social comparison leads to less helpful results. When, for instance, we want to bolster our self-image, we like to compare ourselves with those who are less able than we are; we make downward social comparisons. In such cases, learning has little to do with our motivation; we're simply making ourselves feel good by drawing comparisons with those we deem less able. More important, these comparisons set us up for future unhappiness, because tomorrow we'll surely be faced with someone else who's better than we are.

The problem isn't simply that we are too fond of comparing

ourselves with others; it's as much that the comparisons we make are rarely accurate. The psychologist Mark Alicke has conducted several studies that demonstrate our tendency to exaggerate the abilities of others who are better than we are, a phenomenon he calls the "genius effect."[2] Essentially, he found that we attribute the success of those who outperform us to unique, rare, or exceptional abilities in order to salvage our self-images. After all, we don't look nearly so bad when the other person is "gifted." On those occasions when we come out on top in the comparison, we again exaggerate the difference. This time, we overemphasize our own abilities.

Not only do we exaggerate the abilities of ourselves and others but we don't consider the influence on behavior of the context, which can momentarily enhance or hinder performance. For instance, the other person may not have slept well the night before or her various motivational concerns may affect her performance—perhaps she is not really interested in the task at the moment. We would not expect another person to perform in exactly the same way each time he tried to do something if we thought about it. Nevertheless, our social comparisons often suggest that we are doing otherwise.

To make the comparison, we have to isolate behaviors and treat them as if they are representative of our and others' performance. But behavior fluctuates around its own mean— sometimes we do a little better, sometimes we do a little worse. If you hit a wonderful tennis shot and people compliment you, the compliment might lead you to expect more of yourself than is reasonable. After all, compliments are more likely to be given for atypical performance.

As an aside, this is why we often perform worse after a compliment. It is not that the compliment throws us off but rather that our next shot is likely to be more typical of our ability.

Let's return to social comparison and look at several reasons why they make no sense.

1. Comparisons are evaluative, and as we've observed, evaluations are mindless.

2. Comparisons are based on arbitrary criteria. Which is more important to being a better tennis player: speed, accuracy, grace, or the outcome of the game? Who decided the criteria, and why?

3. Even if we freeze the criteria, the behavior, and the evaluation of the behavior, we have to ask, What was the person's intention in producing the behavior? Was it her best shot, or did she just go through the motions?

4. Even if we knew the intentions and accepted comparisons as evaluative and arbitrary, before we can conclude anything meaningful we should know if the performance was typical or atypical. If it was a splendid performance that was atypical, the next performance may regress to the mean.

5. Comparison ignores the contextual influences on the behavior that are likely to be different the next time. The wind might be from a different direction, the person might be tired, and so on.

This is just a partial list. When we compare ourselves to others, we don't often ask ourselves whether they were performing particularly well at that moment and whether the next time out they are likely to show something different. To make accurate comparisons, we usually need to have much more information than is available to us at any moment.

Giving up our urge to compare is not easy. In fact, the

renowned psychologist Leon Festinger went so far as to say that people have a drive to evaluate their opinions and abilities.[3] When objective means to do so are not available—such as when I want to know whether I'm a good flutist—people compare themselves with others.

A great deal of theory and research has since developed the hypothesis that people make social comparisons to enhance their self-esteem. In particular, Joanne Wood and her colleagues have shown that people make comparisons with others who are inferior or less fortunate than themselves—downward comparisons—in order to feel better about themselves, and comparisons with others who are superior or better off—upward comparisons—in order to motivate themselves or judge their abilities.

I am more likely to compare my tennis with that of someone better than I am than with that of someone I know cannot play as well. As Festinger was quick to note, though, I am not likely to compare myself with those far better than I am. I try, according to Festinger, to close the gap and become as similar to others as I can. There is also a tendency to find ways to reduce any discrepancies between our opinions and those of others. Both of these tendencies—regarding ability and opinion—implicitly reinforce the idea that there is a single view—a right and wrong—and that it is in our best interest to be like everyone else. But who decides on what basis to make the comparison, and who decides the criteria?

We try to teach that we are all alike, especially when we try to reduce prejudice. But we readily notice differences among us, so this approach may be futile. If, instead, we made many *more* distinctions among people, rather than fewer, we could come to see that on some dimensions we are like some people and on others we differ. Thus, if I recognized that I am like John on many dimensions, like Sarah on many others, and like Betsy or

Paul on yet others, the idea of a stable in-group or out-group would have no meaning.

By increasing discrimination—in other words, mindfulness—we may decrease prejudice.[4] By noticing similarities to people now thought of as different from us and noticing differences from people we took to be the same as ourselves, we open up the possibility of not following any one "group" so closely that we lose our individuality, and the possibility of learning from many more sources. Thus, if I identify with one school of art, I may overlook particulars of another that might be more appealing in part, but not whole, for me. Why shouldn't part of the painting, for example, be impressionistic, part representational, and part conceptual, if that helps me express myself? Moreover, if the behavior of John, Sarah, and Betsy can have very different meanings that carry different evaluations, then blanket social comparisons are peculiar at best.

Is there research evidence that we can be completely nonevaluative in this way? I don't know of any. Perhaps Buddha and other spiritual leaders achieved such a state, but most of us have not. We might be less inclined to make social comparisons, however, if we had a better idea of the costs we incur by doing so. Our own research suggests that this is the direction in which we might want to move.

The members of my lab, Judith White, Johnny Welch, Leat Yariv, and I, recently conducted an investigation into the effects of evaluation on negative emotions to see whether frequency of social comparisons, not just their nature, plays a role in well-being.[5] We gave a questionnaire to the participants, men and women aged eighteen to fifty-two, that simply asked them how often they compared themselves with other people on a range of attributes—attractiveness, intelligence, wealth, fitness, and personality—regardless of whether they saw themselves as better or worse than others in those respects. We also gave them a questionnaire that asked how often they expressed various negative feelings and behaviors. We found that those who made frequent social comparisons were also more likely to experience a host of negative feelings than were those who make fewer social comparisons. Those who were less evaluative experienced less guilt, less regret, less blame, and they were also less likely to procrastinate. Moreover, in response to the question "In general, how well do you like yourself?" the group less inclined to make social comparisons liked themselves more.

A follow-up study corroborated these findings. We surveyed police officers about their attitudes concerning security guards, specifically whether the average police officer was superior to the average security guard in a number of areas. Those who were more evaluative had lower self-esteem and less satisfaction in life.

Not only do some draw comparisons less often than others but each of us varies in this regard along our own continuum. That is, we each draw more comparisons at some times than we do at other times, and no one makes social comparisons for every activity in which she or he participates. When we are engaged in an activity we deem unimportant—say, opening a can of soup—we don't worry about whether John or Mary does a better job of it. More important, when we are engaged in any activity, we are absorbed in attending to the aspects of the activity and not evaluating it at all. We may stay evaluative because positive evaluation helps us feel good in the short run. As noted earlier, however, as soon as we agree to accept a positive evaluation as reason to feel good about ourselves, we open the door for the damaging consequences of perceived failure. Depression, suicide, or just feeling bad all result in whole or part from a comparative evaluative stance.

Consider what we actually do when we compare ourselves with someone else. We hold ourselves still, as if we were looking at ourselves in a photograph. In this way we limit the dimensions we measure ourselves on, and forget all the ways we do and can change, making the comparison on an isolated and fixed dimension. To be sure, to measure our intelligence we don't need to consider how attractive we are, but we tend to focus on a single way to understand intelligence. Even though intelligence can, of course, be understood in very different ways, we tend to only look at it in one particular way when we compare our intelligence to someone else's.

Moreover, we ignore the situational constraints that led to our particular behavior. One of the most important findings in social psychology is people's overwhelming tendency to overlook the influences of the situation on their behavior. We tend to think that we are the masters of our fate and that who we are and what we bring to a situation determines how we will behave. But study after study finds that our behavior is largely determined by the situation. The result is that we too often attribute behavior to stable characteristics of a person, what psychologists call "dispositions." Thus, when we look at ourselves the same way an observer would look at us, we are likely to make dispositional attributions for our behavior, that is, believe that the comparison reveals something about the kind of person we are.

Comparing ourselves with other people seems such a natural thing, especially given the subjective nature of our daily experience. How can you know what a grade of C on a test means without knowing what the other students got? How can you know if your painting is any good without looking at those of others? We think we need to look to others because we have no stable, absolute yardstick by which to measure success. And yet, for just this reason, we should be very careful about making these comparisons. We would benefit from being mindful of how the criteria were selected and by whom.

What sense does it make to hold on to an evaluation that we realize is subjective and therefore potentially limiting? How would we have done if different questions had been asked on the test, or if people with different sensibilities had assessed our work? Comparison is especially problematic when we use it to assess not just our performance but our general worth. We tend to make these comparisons without questioning other, potentially meaningful criteria that would have resulted in our different relative standing. That is, by some measures we lose, but just as certainly, by others we would not.

The main reason we don't engage the world more creatively, then, may be that we mindlessly compare ourselves with other people we deem highly creative and we come up short. I've often seen graduate students afraid to start their dissertations because they were comparing the beginnings of their projects with the final results of others. Typically, the problem is with the attribution we make for the difference we observe. If we attribute others' performance to talent, we overlook the work they had to put in and forget that they too had to start at the beginning, with a much less impressive product than the one which so intimidates them now. Perhaps we should ask those with whom we compare ourselves and our work what starting was like for them. We're likely to find out that no one can know in the beginning whether what lies ahead is going to be a great work or an embarrassment.

Starting anything is hard. Having an exaggerated idea about someone else's experience makes it even harder. Starting was so hard for Joan Miró, remember, that he would not paint on a clean canvas. But a soiled canvas, he said, gave him ideas.

The Single Lens of Comparison

*In the perspective of every person lies a lens through which
we may better understand ourselves.*
ELLEN J. LANGER

During the summer I drive from Boston to Provincetown and
back on many occasions. To do so I must drive through Eastham, where a major source of revenue appears to come from
traffic violations. The posted speed limit used to change frequently, ensuring that some would be caught unaware by the
ever-present police, and I have been among that group. Recently
I was pulled over for having changed lanes too often, or so
thought the officer who stopped me. Two weeks later I received
a letter telling me that I must spend a day at a driving school to
avoid a fine. I signed up for the class, which turned out to be the
hardest eight hours I think I ever spent. Yet, in retrospect, it
served a purpose beyond just improving my Eastham driving
behavior.

On the appointed day I drove up to the building and parked
alongside a series of souped up cars belonging to my fellow
classmates. They were all twenty-something males, a tough
crowd, somewhat hostile toward me, although in fact they were
there for essentially the same reason I was. I looked at their
clothes and cars, they looked at mine, and it seemed clear to all
that we were from different worlds.

Just before class began, another woman showed up with her
young daughter. As the class began, the instructor told her the
child was not allowed in the room. She replied that she hadn't
been able to find a sitter and had traveled a good distance to attend the class, but the instructor wasn't sympathetic. Thinking
that the rule was mindless, at least in this case, and after failing
in my initial attempt to persuade the instructor to allow the

child to stay in the room, I proposed an alternative. "Why don't we let the child sit right outside the door, where we can watch her while she draws or plays with her toys to amuse herself?" Even this, however, was not immediately acceptable to the instructor. But then the young men in the class joined my cause and cheered as I continued to argue. I was now one of them, and all of us were "against" her, the instructor. I felt like I was in a scene from *Blackboard Jungle,* although I was not playing my familiar role of teacher. I should point out that eventually the instructor gave in and let the child sit right outside the door.

What fascinated me was how different an experience I had that day because I took the young mother's side instead of keeping quiet. My fellow students saw that I understood the situation from their perspective, and everything I imagined they felt about the system—even the senselessness of much of the day's "lesson"—seemed correct to me. The rest of the day turned out quite different than I thought it would when I arrived. The instructor turned out to be a smoker, and she gave the class regular breaks, allowing me a chance to come to know my fellow students better. And they were now delighted to swap stories with me about why they were in the class, where they lived, and what they did for work. On occasion I was even able to switch roles to the slightly more familiar Mr. Thackeray in *To Sir, with Love* as we talked, offering them advice that was more that of the establishment than that of rebellious outsider.

I spent eight hours that day bouncing between these very different roles, yet they both made complete sense to me and, I think, to my classmates. It was an unusual day. The experience was unusual because we don't often put ourselves in situations with people who aren't a lot like us, although I believe that groups of people who are all alike may not be as much fun. Consider parties. It's reasonable to think that people have parties to have fun. But how many of us typically enjoy parties? If they are designed for fun and yet often are not fun, something must be wrong.

Most parties are homogeneous along the dimensions that matter to the host. The guest list is often constructed to include people of like talent, power, and intelligence, or those from similar areas of interest—academics, musicians, and so on. In fact, the homogeneity of most parties becomes readily apparent after only a few guests arrive. This homogeneity subtly encourages people to be evaluative of themselves and the other guests on whatever the common dimension is. And that's where the problem lies. The fact is, it isn't very much fun to be constantly comparing yourself with others. Recently I held a party to celebrate the reconstruction of my house after a fire, and the nature of that purpose led me to put together a guest list that was quite varied. The party was a surprising success, and later many people remarked to me how much they enjoyed the evening. To my pleasure, one guest, one of my contractors, was the center of attention among several of my academic friends. My guess is that the heterogeneous nature of the guest list contributed to people all allowing themselves to be less evaluative and more authentic. As a result, the party may actually have been fun.

One hypothesis we might draw from these experiences, then, is that the more homogeneous the group, the more its members will use only one yardstick to evaluate themselves and others. If this is true, it casts a new light on the value of diversity. Imagine a cancer support group, for example, composed of patients with the same clinical profile compared with one made up of patients with different profiles and at different stages of the disease. Does the group of patients with similar profiles and a common experience offer stronger support? Someone in the more diverse group may discover that not all members of his group have all the symptoms attendant to the disease, that those who have the same symptoms may have them in varying degrees, and most important, that they may arrive at different solutions to dealing with recovery or treatment. In a sense, the group's variability mimics the individual's possibilities.

The way we are all alike is that we are all different from each other at different times and in different circumstances. And yet, we tend to hold ourselves still and look at ourselves through a single lens when we compare ourselves with others, looking for similarity rather than contrast. When we don't find similarity, we conclude that one of us is better or worse.

Learning from Others

It took me four years to paint like Raphael,
but a lifetime to paint like a child.
PABLO PICASSO

Clearly, some people can draw well and others can't (although, as we'll see, anyone can learn the skills necessary to draw). With that fact in mind, let's compare our drawing ability with that of the Old Masters, a group of artists who can easily make us feel inferior. The artist David Hockney, in his recent book *Secret Knowledge,* tells us that a surprising number of Old Masters used all sorts of optical devices to help them trace the subjects of their paintings.[6] Dürer, Caravaggio, Vermeer, Velázquez, Ingres, and Hals all used such devices. None of which detract from their accomplishment. Hockney tells those who would find the genius of their work diminished:

> *The lens can't draw a line, only the hand can do that, the artist's hand and eye in coordination with his heart. . . . This whole insight about optical aids doesn't diminish anything; it merely suggests a different story.*

The New York Times had a similar story not long ago about Thomas Eakins, who in 1882 was called the "greatest draftsman in America."[7] We now find out that the great Realist "had a secret," that, essentially, he traced from photographs. Yes, some great artists draw brilliantly, and that is wonderful. Millions of dollars, however, have been spent on paintings in which the artists' drawing technique was less central to their appeal.

Comparing ourselves with others in order to try to succeed in exactly the same way they have is a futile task, although looking to other people can show us possibility and opportunity. We may be more likely to say, "Wow, if she can do it, maybe I can too," if we don't make an evaluative upward comparison with those people. It's good to look to others to get information about possibility and the different ways to be successful. But this practice is quite different from deciding that those who've succeeded are in some ways better than we are, or that we are inferior for not having done it. This will be clearer once we examine the myth of talent.

What's more, when we give up social comparisons we may be more likely to recognize how "almost" really *can* count. When we are mindful, and thus process-oriented, components of the task at hand are more apparent. Rather than a mindless "all or nothing" approach, we notice the parts that work and those that may need "rearranging," and the change from failure to success can seem more manageable. We get two benefits from this approach: We learn something that might help our next try, and we don't feel bad about our performance, which itself can detract from future performances. Even when evaluating the other person's performance, if we focus on its components, we can learn more than simply judging whether the person is better or worse than we are.

If I try to produce a work of art just like an Old Master's, it will never be as good as the original, but more important, the journey will be less rewarding. As I've already said, if we know where we are going, we miss half the fun of getting there, but many beginners hold to the belief that looking to others can provide them with a blueprint for success.[8]

Alternatively, we can take the work of other people as a general example of what we might do once we have experience. We might look at a painting by Velázquez, for example, and ask what we would do differently if we were to paint basically the same subject. Not long ago I was in a gallery and was struck by a painting of a single bass swimming across a large canvas. After studying it awhile, I imagined that, if I had painted it, I would have made the eye larger, but I don't mean to suggest that I thought a larger eye would improve the painting. I simply thought it would give the fish a different "personality," one that was more interesting to me. Typically, though, when we make comparisons, we don't do it to gain information; rather we do it to assess our own competence. Of course we all know that we can learn from others. Piet Mondrian learned about taking sensations and turning them into brushstrokes from the Impressionists and Seurat. But, again, comparing ourselves with others to assess our competence, rather than to adjust our skills, limits our competence. Most simply, it does so because in making upward or downward social comparisons we often give up comparisons that could be useful, those focused on gaining information.

In a classic study on our need for affiliation, social psychologist Stanley Schachter led participants to believe they were soon going to receive an electric shock as part of their participation.[9] While they waited for the experiment to proceed, they were given the choice to wait alone, to wait with others about to undergo the same experience, or to wait with others who were not going to have the same experience. Those participants who were expecting the shocks to be painful chose to wait with others about to undergo a similar experience, while the rest had no preference, leading Schachter to conclude that misery loves miserable company. Being with similar others allows us an opportunity to check our emotions and make sure it's okay to feel what we feel. If the participants weren't concerned about feeling the "right" way, they might have found it more freeing to wait with someone who wasn't going to be receiving a shock, an unstressed person who might be a calming influence.

In thinking we see, feel, know, or want the same things as other people, we are led to make mindless comparisons with them. Instead of imagining how you are similar to someone, consider some new ways to envision how the two of you are distinct:

- You may be experiencing the same thing but focused on different aspects of it.

- You may be experiencing the same aspects differently.

- You may be experiencing the same aspects, the same way, yet interpret them quite differently.

The first of these possibilities is reasonably familiar. When a flute player listens to an orchestral piece, the notes played by the flutist may be most salient to him, while a jazz drummer may focus instead on the percussion. The second approach is also familiar to us when the difference is one of evaluation. The optimist sees the glass as half full, the pessimist as half empty. But the third approach, allowing ourselves to interpret the same thing differently, means that I might consider that we both see the glass as half empty but instead of being discontent about it, I may be pleased with the evidence that I've already consumed much of the glass's contents.

If I saw the world from your perspective, would I know how

you feel? Accepted wisdom suggests that I would. But can that be true? There may indeed be a lesson to be learned from walking in someone else's shoes, but I don't believe the walk reveals how another's shoes would feel to him.

In Mark Twain's classic *The Prince and the Pauper,* Prince Edward wants to find out what life is like outside the royal court and switches clothes with the impoverished Tom Canty. Living among the poor, he believes he has learned firsthand what life is like for those far less fortunate than he. Does the prince really have the perspective of a pauper? With his new wisdom, can he rule more justly? To my mind, the answer to the first question is truly no, but the answer to the second may be yes. It depends on what we believe encompasses one's perspective. For me, the worst thing about being a pauper would probably be not knowing if I was going to have enough food to eat or a safe place to live. These are things that Edward, even while playing the pauper, can count on; whenever he wants to change his circumstances, all he has to do is stop trying to take the pauper's perspective and be princely again. Tom, however, does not have this choice.

If perspective is solely the result of being exposed to the same information given in the same way, then all we have to do to understand how someone else might feel is see the information "from her perspective." If, however, the way we understand and feel about information is the cumulative result of our life's experience, then having lived my life and not yours, I cannot ever really know how you feel.

What is to be learned from walking in another's moccasins? Before the walk we may incorrectly believe that we're all alike. Rather than leading us to believe that we can understand another's experience, though, the walk could reveal how much we didn't know beforehand. It could reveal that our own experi-

Sparky, the first painting I entered in a juried show.

Despite my furniture dyslexia, I gave painting furniture another chance.

Two women, content without the burden of social comparison.

My paunchy horse, straddling a fence in a lime green field.

I painted Sparky too small, but it turned out that my "mistake" gave the chair a stronger presence.

Nancy is Southern, so the title of the book seemed fitting. But what is a "Civil War"?

It's clear my engagement with this painting was great fun for me.

I still don't know much about motorcycle engines, but why should I care?

Who says dogs
can't dance?

To my surprise,
taking off paint
was as interesting to
me as putting it on.

I set out to paint us reading, but discovered myself talking—more typical for me.

Knowing there is no risk in trying, I abandoned my usual "style."

As can be seen in the dog's expression, I was engaged but pensive that day.

The context, visiting Buenos Aires, and the movement of the watercolors on the paper determined the content.

The wood that I used to paint on suggested the shapes I "chose."

I realized too late that there was no room for their heads, but the result was more interesting to me.

ence and desires blind us to the differences between us. If we did this often enough, so that we realized how little we know, we'd be more likely to ask people what we want to know and trust their answers. Most important for our present purposes, we'd be freer in our own minds to be ourselves. We'd realize that each of us is the only person we can successfully be. If we are true to ourselves, then we would expect that our art, sport, or work would reflect—indeed celebrate—the differences between us and others. We would follow rules as we learned a new activity, but only as guides, so our idiosyncrasies would be revealed in our behavior.

Countering the Effects of Social Comparison

Every good painter paints what he is.
JACKSON POLLOCK

When I began to paint, I was afraid of what others might think when they compared my work with that of "real artists." When most of us were first exposed to the arts in school, our teachers told some of us that we did not have ability while pronouncing others gifted. We now ought to question what we then took at face value. Why didn't we measure up? With what standards were we implicitly being compared? Was it representational art instead of Impressionism or classical music instead of jazz?

Fabulous Outsider Art, or Brut Art as it is sometimes called, is created by marginal individuals, for example, the mentally ill, criminals, or even children. Their unadulterated work has an authenticity that is often lacking in more "skilled" art, and their very marginality may be responsible for their wonderful creations. Deborah Frable, T. Blackstone, and C Scherbaum have conducted research showing that marginality leads to mindfulness.[10] When we give up the tendency to compare our-selves with others, what remains is our individuality and the present situation in which we find ourselves. This is the perfect recipe for engagement.

Even if it made sense to do so, with whom should we compare ourselves when we want to begin a creative activity? It's hard to know where to start. Jazz, Chinese opera, and a melodic classical symphony are quite different from one another. Renaissance, Cubist, and Brut art are equally different. If we are drawn to something really different, we might even consider Elephant Art.

Elephants have been painting for well over a decade in the United States. Ruby, an elephant from the Phoenix Zoo, had sold more than $500,000 worth of her paintings from the late 1980s when she died in 1998. Inspired by her success, Vitaly Komar and Alexander Melamid opened the first elephant art academy in the world, in Lampang, Thailand; it sells and promotes the paintings of the academy's elephants around the world. The money from the sale of the paintings, fittingly, goes to efforts to preserve and protect the Asian elephant.[11] Suffice it to say that, if "they" can do it, so can we. If a beginning painter feels the need to make comparisons with successful artists, perhaps he should compare himself with these outsiders.

A member of my lab, Laura Delizonna, and I recently conducted a study that investigated the degree to which mindful thinking would minimize the detrimental effects of social comparisons. Of course, our expectation was that more mindful individuals would adopt a nonjudgmental approach to social comparison and that they would be able to consider negative comparisons of their work from other perspectives, improving both their self-esteem as artists and their enjoyment of their art. To encourage a mindful approach to the experience, we gave an explanation of mindfulness to some of the participants, along with instructions for how to use alternate perspectives to rethink negative evaluations.

We asked all the participants to draw a picture of a person. When they were finished, we instructed them to put their drawings in folders. As they did so, some of them found another drawing in the folder, which they were led to believe was the work of a previous participant. Some found a drawing which they were likely to compare unfavorably with their own. Others found a drawing by a highly skilled artist, one with which they would be able to compare their own work only unfavorably. For a third group, there was no other picture in the folder, and thus no comparison would be made. After they had put away their drawings, we had them complete a survey that asked them to rate their work, how much they enjoyed the experience, and how they rated themselves as artists.

When they had finished, we requested that they draw a second picture and again place it in a folder. This time, however, they saw a drawing opposite in skill level from that in the first folder. Again, one group had no drawing in the folder and thus would not make a comparison. After they had completed both drawings, we asked the participants general questions about their drawings and their artistic ability, including comparisons with their usual drawings, potential for improvement with practice, and their artistic ability compared with that of the people generally.

The results were as we expected. The group that felt best about their work was the group that did not make any social comparisons. Of those who were encouraged to do so, participants who took a mindful approach to the unexpected comparison of their work felt better about their work, the experience, and their enjoyment of art in general. Those who saw the poor drawing first and made a mindless downward social comparison that allowed them to feel superior, upon seeing the professional drawing felt the worst about their work and the experience.

Social comparing is one way for us to gain validation. But there are other ways that are not so costly. Because a work of mindful art has so much of the person in it, it is no wonder that artists are eager to show their work and are so disappointed if it does not receive approval. It is hard at that point to separate oneself from the work. Perhaps, rather than looking for positive or negative reactions, in the belief that one person's answer to "do you like it?" has meaning beyond that person's opinion at that moment, we ought to ask more informative questions. What does it mean to you? Would you have added something (or left something out), and why? What does this tell you about me? With these questions, we might learn something about ourselves. As when discussing a dream with a friend, we can exchange insights and, we hope, learn from the experience. Such an exchange should also be beneficial to the friend. If she is helpful, it is probably because of shared experiences. The experience of a shared reality is what is validating to us for the long run, while validation that results from social approval is fleeting.

We search for validation because we know we don't know but mistakenly think there are absolutes that we could know. From the start I painted quickly, the way I'm told I do most everything. I felt insecure when a friend told me how long others took with their paintings until I read somewhere that there are two styles of painters—those who are slow and studied, and those who paint quickly. After reading that I felt validated and believed that I was doing just fine. Now I think back on this concern with amusement; how could it have been any other way? Some of us will obviously paint fast, some slow, and some slower still. Some will paint with the precision of some Japanese artists and others with a desire to capture a fleeting emotion, like the Abstract Expressionists. Some, as I do now, will just paint, fully engaged, not self-conscious, and oblivious to categories and to matters of time.

I was surprised when, several years ago, my dear artist friend Anthony, commented to me on my "style." I had thought that each of my paintings was very different from the next, and he agreed, but he also pointed out ways they were all very similar. I liked the fact that, even though I didn't know what I was doing, I had a style. It made me feel like a "real" artist—whatever that means. Perhaps I shouldn't have been surprised, since what comes through when I am painting mindfully is, of course, myself.

The Experiencing Self

One day seven years ago I found myself saying to myself I can't live where I want to—I can't go where I want to go—I can't do what I want to—I can't even say what I want to . . . I decided I was a very stupid fool not to at least paint as I wanted to.

GEORGIA O'KEEFFE

In his wonderful story "The Mirror Maker," Primo Levi tells the tale of Timoteo, a man who came from a long line of mirror makers. Setting aside the rules of mirror makers, at night Timoteo would try to fashion a mirror to reflect the human mind. After much trial and error, he was able to make one the size of a business card, which when worn on the forehead, revealed to the person looking at it what the wearer saw. He tested it on various people, and when he saw how his wife, Emma, saw him—the way he always wanted to see himself—he realized how dear her love of him was. He distributed his mirrors to many friends and found that no two of them shared the same image of him.

But he could never make money from his extraordinary invention. All the salesmen reported that there were too few customers who expected to be satisfied with their images as reflected on the brows of friends or relations. One hidden cost of making social comparisons is that, if we do it, we are more likely to assume others do as well. We feel judged, and we make this assumption without the use of mirrors.[12]

There are interesting studies showing that we don't compare ourselves with others just to feel good about or assess ourselves. People can seek what they take to be an "accurate" assessment of themselves or they can look for information that is flattering. Much of the time, the search for accuracy and the search for flattery don't conflict. The psychologists William Swann, Brett Pelham, and Douglas Krull, however, have found that people actually may seek negative information about themselves when positive information would be inconsistent with their self-view.[13] Most of the time, however, their research confirms most people's intuition. We choose positive information to enhance our self-esteem. We prefer positive feedback that pertains to our positive self-views but prefer unfavorable feedback regarding our negative self-views. Further, we seek partners who see us as we see ourselves. Thus, those of us with predominantly negative self-views may seek partners who derogate us.

The social psychologists Abraham Tessor and Jonathan Smith have found that people often make comparisons to try to maintain rather than to maximize their self-esteem.[14] They do this by two processes: comparison and reflection. When the comparison is on dimensions that we care about, we compare ourselves with others, but when the characteristics are more or less irrelevant to us, we bask in "reflected glory," e.g., our football team wins and we're happy.

What is very disheartening to me are their findings that

when the dimensions matter to us, we can feel threatened and behave in disappointing ways to bring about a positive comparison. Their research found that when the comparison may prove to be unflattering, we actually interfere with the performance of people close to us so the comparison will be flattering and we can protect our self-esteem. Tessor and Smith had male subjects come to their lab with close friends. Four of them participated as a group—two pairs of friends and two pairs of strangers. One of each pair was to provide clues to the other in what was characterized for some as a game and for others as a test predictive of important verbal skills. Participants gave harder clues to their friends than to strangers when they thought the task to be an important test of verbal skills. When they thought the exercise was just a game, they helped their friends with easier clues.

Herein lies the mindlessness of social comparison. It can lead us to disparage others, interfere with their potential successes, and keep us from engaging in a more creative life out of fear of failure; all in order to protect ourselves. But do we really succeed in protecting ourselves? Ironically, with most of these attempts at self-protection, we hurt ourselves instead. Our concern about self-esteem leads only indirectly to self-protection. If the evaluation of events leads me to feel bad about myself, i.e., hold myself in low self-esteem, then I take steps to protect myself in the future. We accept our search for psychological self-protection as natural because self-protection for our physical selves is taken to be natural. We view potential harm to our physical selves as justification for behavior that otherwise would be unacceptable. In the end, though, psychological self-protection is self-defeating.

Abraham Maslow, most famous for his developmental theory of individual growth, describes several stages through which an individual must progress to reach self-actualization. First we must attend to physiological needs. Once those are met, our concern turns to safety. At this stage in personal development, there is a trade-off between further growth and self-protection. Although he doesn't specify the mechanism, Maslow seems clear in his assumptions that defensiveness halts growth. My argument is that this defensiveness occurs as the result of an evaluative stance. Evaluation is language-based rather than experience-based; the very process of evaluating removes the person from the interaction, that is, from the experience. We seek positive experiences, yet the process of evaluating the experience removes our participation. Defending the self by making downward social comparisons removes the self from the interaction that could provide the opportunity for further growth. The "experiencing self" and the "self-evaluating self" are mutually exclusive, and self-actualization is the antithesis of self-protection.

This may be why, when we look back on the creative process, we frequently feel that we don't know how we did it. When I write, and now when I paint, I am often surprised at the final product. I don't know where it came from. I could worry that I might not be able to do as well ever again, and I might not. But it surely won't happen if I watch, rather than do. We saw earlier that when we repeat a process mindlessly, the resulting products will not be as good as our mindful efforts. We can't and shouldn't know before we begin something where it will end up. All we know is that, once we start, something will result. That is all we need to know. Part of the excitement we experience from creative activities is in seeing what comes to be. If I knew for certain that the next time I play tennis, each shot would be perfect and I was destined to win the point, the game wouldn't be much fun.

The idea that an experiencing self and an evaluating self are

mutually exclusive suggests that, despite our culture's procliv-
ity for "getting in touch with our feelings," there may be an
ironic risk to asking ourselves how we feel. When we are happy,
we tend to go about our business without questioning ourselves. When something happens that leads us to feel bad—we
don't finish the project when we had hoped to, for example—we
compare ourselves with someone else or our ideal self and find
that they have or would have done better. If we let the comparison lead us to question our worth, we may unwittingly begin a
vicious cycle. When we feel good, we don't ask ourselves questions about our self-worth. We just experience ourselves. When
we feel bad, too often those are the very sorts of questions we do
ask. This means in some sense, that the answers we are left with
weigh more heavily than they should. We evaluate ourselves
when we feel bad, we just experience ourselves when we feel
good. So negative information is more available to us in the latter case. If we evaluated ourselves both when we felt good and
when we felt bad, we might have a reasonable way to decide
which feeling is dominant for us. But because the very act of
evaluating reduces our experience, it might be better not to ask.
Instead, we might just let ourselves be.

We are all able to be mindfully engaged, and we can all learn
to avoid making social comparisons. We already do so for matters that we deem unimportant. These are the performances
from which we could learn the most. Creative activities could
serve a similar function, in teaching us to be less evaluative.

We tell our children to be like others, teach them our social
norms. We set up hierarchies and reward some and not others,
suggesting that if they do what others do they will win not only
our approval but material things as well. I can't help but wonder, If children weren't held to one standard, would social comparing be so ubiquitous?

We can be an experiencing self or an evaluative self. The latter requires that we take ourselves out of the experience and hold ourselves still to make the evaluation. If we allowed ourselves just to be our experiencing selves and had some unobtrusive way of making the evaluation, we'd see that there's much more of us.

To my mind, at least part of achieving a personal renaissance is learning to give up our tendency to make social comparisons and to live our lives mindfully.

7

The Myth of Talent

Talent is that which is in a man's power.
JAMES RUSSELL LOWELL

*When my daughter was about seven years old, she asked me one day
what I did at work. I told her I worked at the college—that my job
was to teach people how to draw. She stared back at me,
incredulous, and said, You mean they forget?*
HOWARD IKEMOTO

NOT LONG AGO A FRIEND OF MINE CAME OVER TO DRAW WITH ME.
She had just decided to take up art as a hobby after many years
of wanting to try it but found it more intimidating than inviting. I, of course, wanted to help and encourage her, and I
thought an afternoon drawing and talking would help her relax
and enjoy herself. Looking around for a convenient subject and
finding my dog Gus asleep on the sofa, I suggested that we draw
him. Now I always enjoy drawing and painting Gus, but my
friend soon grew frustrated with her work. It didn't look right
to her, and she tossed the paper away with some exasperation. I
suggested that she try again. When she had finished the new
drawing, she declared that she liked it no more than the first attempt. "I just don't have the talent for this," she protested. This
time I told her to look carefully at her drawing and then look
carefully at Gus, who was still enjoying his nap. Where was
Gus's leg relative to his neck in the drawing? Where was it on

Gus? Try moving the leg down, I explained, and see how much more recognizable he becomes.

When we get something "wrong" and mindfully look to correct what we've drawn, two things happen. First, the drawing improves, and second, we learn more about the subject of the drawing. I now have knowledge to apply as I see fit the next time I draw a dog. "Yes," my friend said softly, "that works, but I still wish I had talent."

While it would be nice if people believed that everyone is talented, most of us are convinced that "either you have it or you don't." That attitude extends even to psychologists, who describe talent as being "normally distributed" throughout the population; that is, a few of us have a lot of it, most of us enjoy an average amount, and a few possess very little. It's a daunting mind-set, one that inculcates in most of us approaching creative endeavors the belief that we belong to the last third of the distribution—we just don't have it.

In fact, in my view, our attitudes about talent are all wrong. For instance, we usually impute to people who are very talented, like Picasso, a knowingness that he wouldn't recognize as he embarked on a new work. It isn't that the talented "know" what they are about to do as much as that they are willing to start something and see where it leads them. We, however, tend to focus on their results and ignore the struggles, uncertainties, and false starts. And so the gap between us widens, although the real difference between those we think of as talented and ourselves may be nothing more than their willingness to go forward in the face of the uncertainty, if only because they believe in the skills they know they can bring to bear.

I recently painted Sparky, Nancy's Jack Russell, riding a motorcycle with Girlie, my West Highland terrier riding on the back. Painting the motorcycle was easy until I got to the engine and realized that I had no idea what a motorcycle engine looks like. Now the choice was to stop painting and find a motorcycle or just make it up. I chose the latter. Sometimes, all we learn is that we don't know. Even those who are "talented" can't paint an engine if they don't know what it looks like.

Is It Talent or Skill?

*If people knew how hard I worked to get my mastery,
it wouldn't seem so wonderful at all.*
MICHELANGELO

The truth is that much of what we ascribe to talent arises from a set of skills that can be learned. Moreover, all of us have a surprising number of skills we have learned in the course of our daily lives, and we are far more prepared to engage in creative endeavors that require talent than we think.[1]

At the moment any of us set out to create something new, we cannot know if what we are about to do will work or not. That's just as well, for if Picasso had known exactly what he was going to paint and how it would be received before he started, he probably would have become bored with painting. If each time Tiger Woods swung a club he had no doubt that the ball would land in the cup, he probably wouldn't enjoy golf at all. Instead, as he chooses the best club to hit a one-hundred-yard approach shot, he has to imagine how essentially the same swing will work now that he is playing the fifteenth hole, more tired than when he faced a similar shot on the fifth. He must take into account that although the wind today is similar, it is not exactly the same as the last time he played this course. Even the fit and feel of his shoes are not exactly as they were yesterday. All of these differences, and countless others, add to the uncertainty of what will happen when he hits the ball. When we think about it a bit, we can understand that even the talented do not "know" exactly what they will do or if it will work. Instead, they begin and see where it leads them, and therein lies all the fun.

I have long enjoyed going to museums, but until I started painting myself, I never thought I could do anything that required artistic talent. I would consider the paintings that hung in museums and galleries, and imagine that the artists all possessed enormous talent, as if there were one particular set of skills and abilities that enabled us to be artistic. I lumped all the talents of all artists together, compared them with my own abilities, and naturally judged myself deficient. The fact is, I didn't understand what it takes to be an artist. Now I look at how very different artists are, and I see an array of abilities. Paintings by Mondrian or Miró may require a different definition of talent than paintings by Rembrandt or Picasso.

When we think about trying something for the first time, we typically understand it only in vague, abstract terms. If that's the case, why should we worry about our ability to do something before we know anything about it? Our lab once conducted a simple study that asked artists and nonartists what they thought it took to be a successful artist. The nonartists pretty much believed that you have to be able to draw; they were able to articulate only a few skills they thought necessary, while the artists had longer lists. The average number of skills listed by the nonartists was 2.7, versus 4.5 for the artists. Most participants listed vague abstractions like "creativity" and "imagination." In fact, only one person among the nonartists mentioned anything even reasonably concrete. In contrast, 64 percent of the artists had specifics on their lists, including eye-hand coordination, an understanding of color and space, and a sense of symmetry and balance. Several in this group also mentioned "patience," but all listed abilities that many of us who have never picked up a paintbrush may in fact possess.

If we asked engineers what it takes to do "engineering," they'd be likely to offer specifics that those of us who are not engineers would not even know to consider. The same is true for virtually any profession. There are, of course, types of work for which we believe we have a good idea of the necessary skills, because we have experiences every day with those who do the job, such as teachers or policemen and policewomen. Still, if any of us were asked to step in and do one of these jobs, I think we'd soon realize that our knowledge about the job requirements is actually quite limited.

With almost any creative endeavor, we mistakenly think that we know what translates into success, and it's usually what we know that keeps us from trying ourselves. When we gave the artists' lists to those who believed that they weren't artistically talented and asked how many of the skills they felt they could do, everyone checked off a few and many checked off most. Not understanding the skills professionals deem important does not mean that we couldn't be successful ourselves if we gained experience. If you have never gardened, you probably wouldn't know how to use many of the garden tools I see my in my neighbor's yard. If you've never made up an exam for introductory psychology students, you would not be likely to know how many questions are needed for an hour-long exam. The real problem isn't that we don't know these things. Our problem is that we *think* we should know without that which only firsthand experience can teach us. And this negative expectation leads us to shun activities that we would find satisfying if only we gave them a fair try.

Our admiration of the result—the great painting, the inspiring performance, the perfect approach shot—ignores the process—the struggles, uncertainties, and false starts that even "the talented" confront. Even when we acknowledge them, we tend to minimize the difficulties, to admire how easy some are able to make it look. And so we ever widen the gap between them and us, and obfuscate the fact that the products of what we assume to be talent spring mostly from skills that can be learned.

If we believe talent is a birthright, then either we have it or we don't. If we see it as a skill, then talent can be learned. I'll add an alternative notion here that I think is worth considering. When we allow ourselves to be fully in the moment—those times that, in retrospect, we feel we were totally absorbed in an activity, a channel for the creative flow without any "self" getting in the way—we are probably our most talented selves.[2]

The Steps to Talent

Talent can't be taught, but it can be awakened.
WALLACE STEGNER

If I were to paint a flower and then decide that my painting looks very little like a flower, what should I conclude? Many would suggest that I simply don't have a talent for painting flowers. But I think that's wrong. It's not that I don't have the talent, it's that I don't yet know the subtleties of flowers. I haven't yet learned enough about them to capture them in a painting, or my view of flowers is different from that of other people. I could represent another view of flowers, however, if I set my mind to it.

It's knowing that there are steps to learning anything, especially creative endeavors—painting, playing an instrument, or writing well—that is the key. Students often come to my office to chat, but they are easily intimidated when they find themselves in their professor's office. If, in conversation, I suggest that I find a particular theory "arcane" and the student isn't sure of the word's meaning, I often sense that the student now presumes I must know every word in the English language. He might now hesitate in choosing his words, unsure that he is using them correctly. Our conversation becomes careful, hesitant. But what if he were to notice a dictionary on my desk opened to a page with the heading "Ar"? He might just as well conclude that I had only recently learned the meaning of the word, that my vocabulary was learned, and that he too could learn it. The conversation then would become, I think, much more relaxed and open. When the steps to accomplishing something are hidden from us, we assume "they" just know it, or "they" can just do it. Even if a propensity for language, art, sports, and so on were genetically determined, the gifted individual still has to learn the particulars. The gap between the talented and the not talented is usually in the particulars, not in some inherited quality that's inaccessible to the rest of us.

If too many of us hold back from doing things because we imagine that we have no talent, if ignoring the particulars only makes us blind to the process of talent, we have a lot of help, especially with respect to art, music, and literature, from critics who widen the gap considerably.

To read art historians, one would think that all the great artists were intent on making political statements about their times, keenly aware of complex scientific ideas, and certainly able to articulate their awareness of color, light, and other technical aspects of their art. In fact, many artists just paint without much regard to such grand ideas. Viewers are entitled and indeed should be encouraged to find in an artwork what is meaningful to them, but it will not necessarily reflect the artist's intention. Magritte aside, if I paint a cigar, I may well have just wanted to paint a cigar. But a critic might say that I painted the cigar to have the viewer question whether a cigar is just a cigar, imbuing the painting with great psychological meaning, since after all, the artist in this case is also a psychologist.

Whenever we look back at the work of others, we seem to overlook the smaller steps. In fact, we even lose them when we look back at our own efforts. As we go forward in life, we focus on the details of everyday living to lead us through the day. The typical day ahead is a series of steps, tasks, or activities that call for our attention. When we look back on what we did, however, we tend to impose grand, often moral explanations on our behavior. The details get lost when we look back, washed away in favor of large, abstract explanations. These abstractions get us into trouble, because as my mentor, Robert Abelson, was fond of saying (and it seems I am too), *while it is easy to find reasons for what we do, it is hard to do what we find reasons for*. The problem with creating these explanations is that we unnecessarily lock ourselves into rules for our behavior that limit us, or even make us feel like hypocrites, when we are inclined to act differently later. Moreover, such explanations lead us to be evaluative of anyone who behaves differently from us.

The imposition of grand explanations for our actions or those of others can have similarly negative consequences. Paintings, symphonies, and essays are created, after all, because that's what artists, composers, and writers do. As the British composer Elisabeth Lutyens once said in response to those who accused her of being too prolific, "They want you to write one masterpiece. I have an eighteenth-century view. A dog barks and a composer composes." (It is interesting to note that this extremely talented composer was given a violin to play at nine years old to cure her nail biting. She devoted herself to music not because of any natural talent—no one in her family apparently knew anything about music—but because of a wish for privacy.)[3] The distance between those who do and those who don't is not as great as it feels to those who want to but are afraid to. The abstractions that critics attach to artists and their work more often than not lead many of us to feel more intimidated. Ironically, they increase the gap that lies between us and the artist, when their role is usually presumed to be that of bringing us closer to the artist and her art.

Blind to the situational forces on us and other people, we too readily attribute stable dispositions to them. Dr. Lewis Fraad tells a story that Hemingway wrote about during the Spanish Civil War. The commanding officer ordered the Lincoln Brigade volunteers to take cover to avoid enemy fire, but one soldier, Dr. William Pike, didn't. As a result, he was able to spot the precise location of the enemy, which turned out to be crucial in winning the battle, and Pike was rewarded with a medal for his courage. When asked why he didn't duck like the others, he replied, "I'm hard of hearing, so I didn't hear the command."

I recently read about and attended an exhibition at Harvard of paintings by Piet Mondrian that focused not on abstract explanations of his work but on his process of creating them, supplying the details that usually get forgotten. It was a most unusual approach to Mondrian and his work. Influential critics such as Clement Greenberg and Rosalind Krauss have usually emphasized Mondrian's idealist side, his evocation of a world of pure mind, whose relation to his paintings resembles that of Plato's ideal forms to everyday reality. In fact, Mondrian, through his own writings and lifestyle gave credence to this interpretation. In an essay on his work, he spoke of an "absolute harmony of straight lines and pure colors underlying the visible world." That's a pretty daunting price of admission for any of us interested in exploring painting. But Harry Cooper, associate curator of modern art at Harvard's Fogg Art Museum, and Ron Spronk, at the Straus Center for Conservation, decided to focus the exhibition on *how* Mondrian created his paintings. Cooper explained in an interview that "we wanted to show that [Mondrian's paintings] are not just designs or diagrams of a higher reality."

Cooper and Spronk's strongest argument for developing a new understanding of Mondrian comes from the laboratory. Their examination of the paintings went far beyond the capacity of the naked eye, encompassing X-ray, ultraviolet, infrared, and microscopic photography. These techniques allowed them to penetrate below the surface of the paintings and to make deductions not only about the changes Mondrian made but also about the order in which he made them. In many cases the curators were able to compare their findings with photographs of the paintings in Mondrian's Paris studio, adding a further dimension to the study.

Their research makes clear that Mondrian's method for reworking the paintings was intuitive and exploratory. He did not follow any preconceived philosophical or mathematical principles but rather composed by eye, trying one change and then another. If his only concern had been abstract design, then painting over his earlier work would have been an acceptable way of presenting new ideas, but this was not how Mondrian proceeded. Before adding a new area of color, he detached the canvas from the stretcher and laboriously scraped away the old paint in that spot, then built up the surface again.

"It was a quite physical, almost violent process of revision," Cooper said. Close-up photos of the paintings show not the smooth, featureless surface one might expect if Mondrian's chief concern had been to convey a disembodied world of shapes but a highly textured field of brushstrokes, some short, some long, angled in different directions as well as cross-hatched.

Like all of us, Mondrian painted step-by-step, despite how he or anyone else might describe his work after it was completed.

The Control of Talent

It doesn't make much difference how the paint is put on as long as
something has been said. Technique is just a means
of arriving at a statement.
JACKSON POLLOCK

Beyond keeping us from creative involvement, the myth of talent frequently leads many of us to abandon prematurely the creative activities we take up. When our initial results don't show much promise, we conclude, "I just don't have a knack for this." We are forgetting that we can learn to do most anything.

Wendy Smith and I recently conducted a rather simple but perhaps important study on talent. We recruited participants who felt they had no artistic talent and asked them to draw a face. Before they began, we gave one-half of them a few rules of anatomy—telling them that typically the distance between the eyes and the top of the head is about the same as the distance between the eyes and the chin. (Van Gogh, it turns out, didn't know this relationship when he began painting.) We didn't offer the second half any assistance.

After they had finished their drawings, we asked both groups to draw a second face, then another, three in all. When the drawings were complete, we gave the participants a question-naire to see how they assessed their ability. The results were quite interesting. Not surprisingly, those who were not given any assistance felt that drawing required skill they didn't possess. Those given some information, however, felt that their drawings showed steady improvement. Nevertheless, the mindset for talent is so strong that even in the face of this improvement they clung to the belief that drawing requires talent.

There are rules to any "game," and learning them makes the doing that much easier. But as we learn them we need to remember that any endeavor requires an attitude like that of the British theatrical producer and director Peter Brook: "A play is an exact set of rules. And yet the playing is a complete circulation around these rules."[4]

I enjoy singing and do so quite frequently. I have often noted to myself that when I'm imitating Maria Callas or Barbra Streisand I am more likely to sing on key than when I just sing. To be sure, I would be happy if I sang on tune more of the time (as would those within earshot), but I am not at all saddened by not being an accomplished singer. Since I sing often and enjoy it, it does not seem sensible to say that I just don't care about singing, as researchers studying self-esteem might conclude.

Other researchers would say singing is just not part of my self-concept, yet there is nothing in my behavior that would indicate this. During summer months at casual parties that end up in song, I frequently sing solo and play the part of the "moving ball," trying to stay just ahead of the music to provide the words for those who don't know them. I can differentiate between melodic voices and my own. I simply accept the way I sing. Because of this acceptance, I am able to sing without being evaluative of myself or concerned with what others think. I believe I could learn to sing better, so my acceptance is not based on any idea about talent or limits regarding what can be learned. Nor is it based on resignation. I am not resigned to the belief that I cannot sing very well, and I'm not committed to any particular belief about my voice in the future. Just being nonevaluative allows me to sing unabashedly. Our singing, just like our drawing, can be improved if we desire to do so and attend to the smaller parts of the task, for instance, the notes we can hit or the ways we can "phrase" the words to suit our voices. But most of us don't typically take the opportunity very often or try to improve if we believe singing requires talent.

We can break any accomplishment down into smaller parts until it becomes more manageable. Likewise, virtually any talent can be broken down into small enough pieces that most of us can learn it. If we believe we may be able to learn it, there is reason to try. If we believe that one either has the talent or doesn't, and that we belong in the latter group, trying would be pointless. Is there any sure way of knowing if we can do something or not? If we try and achieve a modicum of success, then we have evidence that we can learn it. If we fail, all we can know is that there is no evidence that we can learn it, *but it is not evidence that we can't.*

This discussion raises a larger issue that is very important to our trying anything new: *Things are either controllable or indeterminate. We cannot know if something is uncontrollable.* All we can know is that it has not yet been controlled. Tomorrow will show that at least some of what we take as impossible today is indeed possible, it's just that the particular way had not yet been found. Thus, *uncontrolled* does not mean "uncontrollable."

Let's take a closer look at what *uncontrollable* means with the hope that we will question what we now mindlessly accept as beyond our reach. What do people typically mean when they declare an outcome uncontrollable? "I couldn't paint, sing opera, write a great novel, et cetera, if my life depended on it," or so we prematurely conclude. We simply cannot know if that is true. We used to believe that a woman over fifty could not have a baby—it simply was out of her control. Today we know that not only can she conceive but she may be able to determine the baby's sex.

Think of what we take to be chance-determined events to make the point even more convincing. A chance-determined outcome is one for which we do not, at present, have the means of specifying the conditions necessary to produce a particular outcome systematically. This does not mean that the conditions are unspecifiable. When we say that coin tossing is chance-determined, we should perhaps be saying that in the past and at the present time our knowledge of the factors that control the outcome is insufficient. To figure out the bias of the coin would take so many tosses that we don't want to bother, and so we say it is chance-determined. But does it seem so far-fetched to assume that a machine could be built that took into account factors such as the mass of the coin, gravity, and the conditions of the air, so that which side of the coin was originally face up would basically determine the outcome of the toss? And if the machine could be created, could we not learn which factors are most important since we are designing the machine and, with much practice, come to be able to mimic the machine some of the time?

Take roulette as another example. What would it take for a roulette wheel to be manufactured so that each number is precisely equal to every other one? That would mean that in transit the balance of the wheel doesn't change and the use of the wheel is such that each time it spins it does so without affecting this precision. Without such precision, there will be bias in the wheel. Again, discovering this bias would take too many trials to make it worthwhile. But that is a very different thing than the presumption that there is no bias.

Can anyone paint? Either we can or we don't know if we can.

It's not sensible or useful, however, to say we cannot. Is horse racing chance-determined? No more or less than people racing is. Any activity can be reduced to chance by ignoring (or not searching for) those factors that systematically vary. The question becomes whether or not it is productive to search for those factors. In a discussion between Erwin Schrödinger and Niels Bohr about wave mechanics, Schrödinger objected, "Surely you realize that the whole idea of quantum jumps is bound to end in nonsense." To which Bohr replied, "What you say is absolutely correct. But it does not prove that there are no quantum jumps. It only proves that we cannot imagine them, that the representational concepts with which we describe events in daily life and experiments in classical physics are inadequate when it comes to describing quantum jumps. Nor should we be surprised to find it so, seeing that the processes involved are not the objects of direct experience."[5]

It would seem that any advance, personal or scientific, depends on the assumption that what is not yet known is knowable. If I told you that I believe limbs which have been severed can regenerate, could you be sure they can't? It's hard to imagine, primarily because it hasn't happened yet. What if in 1798 an individual told you he thought he could figure out how to fly? Clearly this too would have been hard to imagine if our view were prospective rather than retrospective. Wouldn't it seem that something presumably as permanent as brain damage is clearly uncontrollable? Nevertheless, recent evidence suggests that brain damage suffered by chronic alcoholics may in fact be reversible.[6] Any consideration of history allows us to see case after case in which what was presumed to be uncontrollable became controlled. But certainly this would not prove that all is potentially controllable. And certainly it would not prove that we can do that activity for which we're sure we have no talent.

However, by the same token, descriptions of actions not known to exist that lead to the assumption of uncontrollability do not *prove* uncontrollability.

Of course, we don't have to believe we can master an activity to enjoy it, but let's stay with this argument for a bit longer. Some of the alleged dangers of perceiving control in "uncontrollable" situations are that it wastes our time and effort and keeps us from more productive enterprises; that "inevitable" failures will lead to perceived incompetence and helplessness; or that believing that all situations are controllable leads to excessive self-blame when the situations, "in fact," are not controlled. While it may be argued that all these alleged dangers are reasonably, or at least statistically, related to perceived control, they are by no means necessary consequences of that perception.

To perceive control with respect to some goal does not mean that one must attempt to exercise it in pursuit of the goal. Nor does it mean that one has responsibility for exercising it. After consideration, one may easily decide that the goal is not worth expending all the time and effort deemed necessary to achieve it. Furthermore, beginning on a path does not necessitate staying on it. I like painting in the style that is a blend, perhaps, of Folk Art and Impressionism, but I might decide to try painting with great realism. If I try and I don't succeed at first, that is not an indication that I cannot do it. The judgment about when and if to terminate effort and apply it elsewhere is independent of the perception of control. Such termination, however, clearly need not mean that the person must now perceive uncontrollability; it is simply an individual judgment that time and energy would be more satisfactorily spent elsewhere—perhaps in pursuit of some other goal.

Psychologists have argued that the individual who tries to attain the unattainable and gives up will suffer from self-recrimination.[7] The comparison implicitly being made is between giving up with respect to one goal and succeeding with respect to another. Now clearly, success is typically a more positive experience than failure. This isn't the appropriate comparison, however, and there is no logical reason to assume that giving up along the way leads to more self-recrimination than giving up initially ("Why did I waste my time?" versus "Why didn't I at least try?"). Furthermore, success at difficult tasks is usually more rewarding than successes that are easily achieved, making the effort worth it.[8] We can never know in advance whether success will occur, we may know only that we have no personal precedent for success.

Many of the limits we impose on ourselves are illusory, but can we really overcome them? In a study I conducted in 1983 with students Joel Johnson and Howard Botwinick, we attempted to extend some self-imposed limits.[9] Our research strategy was to investigate whether mindfully focusing subjects on the process by which a problem might be solved (a "process orientation") would be more successful than having them look to the anticipated outcome of an attempt to solve the problem (an "outcome orientation"). The difference between an outcome orientation and a process orientation can be conceptualized as the difference between mindlessness and mindfulness.

The participants, all Harvard students, received written instructions informing them that the study was going to examine their reactions to a problematic situation likely to occur in daily life. All subjects read a written description of one of six problems, in paragraphs of one hundred to two hundred words. The situations covered a range of personal and interpersonal problems—somewhat difficult, but by no means impossible, to solve. Subjects were asked to imagine themselves in one of the following situations:

1. Facing an imminent attack by bounding Doberman pinschers

2. Participating as the third member of a committee on which the other two members harbor sharp antagonism toward each other

3. Being asked to memorize the names of forty-five class members on the first day of psychology class

4. Attempting to go to sleep the night before a statistics final after retiring late and feeling tense, irritated, and ill-prepared

5. Soliciting a charitable contribution from an elderly gentleman shortly after experiencing a near collision with him in heavy traffic

6. Attempting to approach an attractive but aloof stranger of the opposite sex at a party

After they had read a description of one of these situations, we asked the participants to outline the strategy or strategies they might employ to cope with it (the action or actions they might take that would enable them to achieve the goal) and then estimate, on a scale of zero to one hundred, their likelihood of being successful. Half of the subjects were requested to describe their strategies for coping before knowing that they would be asked to estimate their likelihood of success (the process-oriented group), while the remaining half were requested to estimate their likelihood of success before knowing that they would be asked to describe their strategies (the outcome-oriented condition).

We were, of course, more interested in both groups' estimates of their likelihood of successfully solving the problem than in their particular solutions. Those participants who had been given a process orientation expected much greater success

than those for whom we had encouraged an outcome orientation. Subjects who listed strategies first had solid grounds for
greater confidence in their ability to solve the problems, and
those who estimated probabilities first probably underesti-
mated their capacity. But without trying, how could one know
if she could succeed?

We tested the effect of a process orientation in another experiment that examined a different mechanism by which our
perceived limitations might be extended. In this study, we asked
one group of participants to find as many solutions as they
could think of for problems that we posed.[10] We took the average number of solutions per problem from this group and
asked a second group to find at least that number plus five. This
group was able to give far more solutions than the first. In one
instance, the "find as many as you can" participants gave us an
average of 6.7 solutions while the second group averaged 16.2. In
another instance, the first group found 9.0 solutions compared
with 21.5 for the second.

These results have intriguing implications for the study of
control. They indicate that perceived limitations on capacity
may, at least on occasion, be overcome by an instruction that fo-
cuses on methods of solving the problem at hand rather than
on the participants' evaluation of whether they thought they
could solve the problem. Similarly, improvement may be found
by giving an instruction that merely presupposes a higher capacity than the person thought she was capable of. These participants generated more solutions of equivalent quality when
merely told to list a higher number. It seems a rather safe assertion that appraisals of personal capacity made after consideration of a wider base of information—that is, after reviewing the
strategies that might be used to solve the problem—are probably more valid than estimates made before such consideration.

The Power of Thinking Mindfully

When you are writing before there is an audience anything written is as important as any other thing and you cherish anything and everything that you have written.
GERTRUDE STEIN

Most of us, on the brink of trying something new, are likely to ask "Can I do it?" But for all of us the question "How do I do it?" is a better place to start. It's my belief that the major difference between those "that can" and those "that can't" may be not much more than the number of attempts the former group has made.

Successful popular psychology authors like Norman Vincent Peale have long maintained that one should constantly "think success" as a means of attaining it. Peale advised us to continually "precondition" our minds to success, to "forecast that you are going to achieve a certain goal and then move steadily toward that goal." Our experiments, in contrast, indicate that the goal may be better served by dwelling on the means. This may be particularly true of individuals who are prone to worry that they cannot achieve the goal—that is, the very individuals who are often alleged to need "success conditioning" the most. If we cannot be certain that we can or cannot learn any particular talent, our studies suggest that just believing that talent is not the issue increases the chances that we will start to engage ourselves instead of hesitating.

Everything we have experienced is part of who we are and will affect everything we try in our own unique way. If we use what we already know and apply it to our new activity, we may find we bring to the activity what is perhaps the most important quality to creative endeavor: originality. The artist Wassily Kandinsky was also a social scientist; the biologist Desmond

Morris was also a painter; the musician Charles Ives was also an insurance agent; Sofya Kovalevskaya, the renowned mathematician, was also a playwright; the poet William Carlos Williams was also a physician; the poet E. E. Cummings was also a painter; Sir Ronald Ross was a physician, scientist, composer, and poet but best known for his work on malaria. These and many others like them may have excelled precisely because they brought their past training to bear on their creative pursuits and vice versa.

Many of us don't see the relevance of our past accomplishments to a new activity. Yet, if we were to break up most pursuits into smaller components, we'd find many similarities between what we already know and what is required. Teachers and lawyers, for example, are clearly in different professions. Yet in their work both write, read, persuade, summarize, engage in meaningful interactions with people, and so on. Indeed, as we saw at the beginning of this chapter, when artists described what it takes to create good art, many of those who think they lack the talent to be artists find that they have quite a few of the requisite skills.

Consider all the mundane activities in which we engage that are so much more creative than we give them credit for. Putting on makeup or picking out which clothes to wear is often a highly creative act. Even some men I know who would never consider themselves creative shave creatively, moving the razor subtly this way or that to create a new look for the day. The same is true for picking out furniture or colors for the house, planning which flowers or plants will be aesthetically pleasing, and so on.

The skills we have for one activity are often like those used in other activities, but we don't realize it. In the movie *The Karate Kid,* the master has the student wax his car, paint his fence, and then sand the floor. The adolescent, eager to learn karate, gets annoyed at what he thinks are irrelevant tasks, objects to doing more, and then is shown how he has just learned a good deal of karate by transferring his waxing, painting, and sanding to the martial arts.

When we speak of talent we rarely define the dimensions or components about which we are speaking. In this way we make a talent seem more general than it might be, and the rest of us less talented by comparison. That's even the case when we consider the genius. Genius at what? Would Mozart have been able to compose great music if he had been born and raised in China, where atonal sounds are appreciated? If Picasso had been born Balinese, would there have been a point to his art? To be talented in art means what? Consider Picasso, Matisse, Pollock, Miró, Mondrian, and Rembrandt. They are all thought to be very talented, but their work has little in common. When we say we have no talent for art, with whom are we comparing ourselves? John Donne was a very cerebral poet; E. E. Cummings was wonderfully playful; and Emily Dickinson mostly emotional. When we say we can't write poetry, with which of these talents are we comparing ourselves? The music of John Cage is quite different from that of Mozart, whose music hardly bears a resemblance to Chinese opera. Tiger Woods, Serena Williams, and the jockey José Santos use different muscles in different ways, yet they are all great athletes. Each of these domains—art, poetry, music, and sport—is multidimensional. To our detriment, we tend to reduce them to a single understanding when we speak of the talent they require.

A friend of mine saw some of my early paintings when visiting me at home. Later that night she remarked to me, "There is something to your art." Then she warned, "Now, don't go thinking you're Rembrandt." I'm not sure what the warning was for, but all I thought when she made it was that, similarly, *Rembrandt wasn't me.* I knew if I spoke it that she would not understand it as I meant, so I kept silent. If I am true to my life's experience and I paint mindfully, no one else can do my particular painting better—that is, no one else can better represent *me* than I can. That authenticity is all I seek in my painting. If I am authentic, I am necessarily original. Will there be an audience that appreciates the originality? Yes or no, but that question doesn't speak to whether there is talent operating. Even those who today we are certain were talented—for instance, Manet, van Gogh, or Pollock—had no audience at first. In fact, each new movement in art—or for that matter, the beginning of any paradigm shift in any discipline—is at first rejected. Would we want to say these artists were not talented because they lacked audience appreciation? Of course not, yet many of us consider their works and can only feel inferior by comparison. As we will learn, we now see their talent because of the ways we were taught to see, not because it is a foregone conclusion that they were talented or, more precisely, that we are not.

Let me make an extreme assertion: *Everybody has an equal talent for everything.* We may differ in the particulars that suit our unique experiences and in the degree of appreciation we earn from our audiences. If we look beyond mere talent, it is interesting to consider that even the theories of most geniuses were rejected in their day. Did they not have any talent when they were unappreciated? Audience appreciation, after all, is psychologically determined to a large part. It is one part conformity, one part a willingness to engage the stimulus, one part the *context* in which the work is viewed, one part the mindfulness of the viewer, and finally, of course, some aspect of the work itself.

The real problem with taking too seriously the idea of talent as being normally distributed among people is that, if we find ourselves on the wrong end of the curve, we just assume we don't have what it takes. By definition, "everyone can't be great at something" if we think that is so. No, everyone can't be equally great if we hold still a single criterion for evaluation. But criteria can and do vary. By making a personal attribution that we don't have talent, we accept mediocrity and feel bad that we do not excel rather than find the way we could excel. Our focus on talent, in fact, leads us to tend to think of ourselves as fitting on an even more vague normal distribution in life. We tend to believe we are extremely competent, moderately competent, or extremely incompetent.

Even if we accept the conventional view of talent, it doesn't matter whether we are talented or not. The reason to engage in any creative activity is that to do so is to feel alive and in turn to become enlivened. Will anyone really think less of us if we just can't paint, sing, or write, very well? Probably not.

If I try, and fail, am I any worse off? It is an interesting exercise to attempt to do things we think we can't do, but would like to try just for fun. If we don't globalize the result and conclude "I can't paint (or more global still, I can't do anything artistic) because I can't draw *this* dog," for example, what is lost? Whose affection is at risk? What opportunity that we've counted on will not be ours? Someone might point out that these examples are mere avocations, so with them there's not much at stake. Fine, now do the same exercise with matters we take to be more serious. The results are not all that different.

To my good fortune, I've never thought to ask myself whether I have the talent to do something. If the activity—academic, artistic, or physical—seemed interesting, I tried it. If I didn't quite get it, I tried it differently. Why should I know how to do something I've never done before?

It is odd to me that so many people feel they aren't artistic when we can't even agree on what art is. This is one of those questions about which too many books are written. In 1995 Vitaly Komar and Alexander Melamid, Russian emigrant artists, began a project that set out to discover the Most Wanted, as well as the Least Wanted, paintings. Interested in finding a true "people's art," they posted digitized versions of the paintings on the Internet and invited the visitors to their website to take a market survey questionnaire on their artistic preferences. Over 3,000 people completed the online survey, after which Komar and Melamid studied the preferences of people in more than a dozen countries, creating Most Wanted and Least Wanted lists for each country. It is interesting that, while they sought to find agreement across cultures, tastes varied so widely that no definition of art even within a culture could be discerned.

In 1998 the Guggenheim Museum in New York had a show entitled The Art of the Motorcycle, in which one hundred motorcycles were displayed. The Brooklyn Museum has a Cranston toy robot on display, and the films featuring the Claymation characters Wallace and Gromit have been shown at Boston's Museum of Fine Arts. And, of course, we are all aware of Andy Warhol's Campbell's soup cans. Critics accuse those responsible for such displays of dumbing down art. My view is otherwise. It would be nice if, after seeing exhibitions like these, we realized that anything can be art. Indeed, it is to our advantage to see the art in everything.

If we did, I believe it would be easier to see how we may all be artists. How much simpler it would thus be to live the artful life.[11]

8

The Blindness of Knowing

Art does not render the visible; it makes visible.
PAUL KLEE

I love Paris in the
the springtime.
COLE PORTER

LOOK AT THE LINE FROM COLE PORTER ONCE MORE. IT'S SUCH A familiar phrase that most of us miss the repetition of the word *the*. We know the expression so well, in fact, that we don't really need to "read" the line, so we hardly look at it. If vision is our most developed sense, here is a vivid example of how we mindlessly exercise it, not seeing the world around us because we think we already know what it contains.

Gertrude Stein told us that "a rose is a rose is a rose." But in learning the ways that all roses are alike, we run the risk of becoming blind to their differences. With all due respect to Gertrude Stein, a rose is *not* a rose is *not* a rose. It is certainly easier to talk about roses if all their subtleties are ignored, but then our reactions to them become dull, oblivious to the finer distinctions we could have drawn. When we attempt to draw a rose or write a poem about a rose, these subtle, individuating properties become important. When we want to appreciate the gift of a single rose, they might be important as well. This rose *is* different from other roses and is itself different when seen from other perspectives and at other times.

In order to simplify interpersonal communication, we use language in ways that effectively direct our attention to a level of abstraction which enables us to communicate easily. We talk about a rose as though we all experience the same flower in the same way. Our everyday language directs us to similarities, not differences. That language, however, leads us to accept all that the abstraction entails and to ignore all that appears irrelevant to the general case. We distinguish a rose by observing how it is like the other flowers we call roses, and we mindlessly react to it much the same way each time.

The opportunity for creating new choices for ourselves comes only when we are open to noticing the very differences that work against this tendency. If the gloss of interpersonal communication tends to deflect us from a richer personal experience, I am not going to argue that we should ignore the ways the world is similar and focus only on the differences. That would be foolhardy. It's nice to recognize that a sound is a bird's song even without knowing which bird's. It is nicer still, however, to be able to recognize the species, perhaps even the particular member of that species. We do this with the voices of our friends and movie stars and singers. My suggestion is that as we learn to generalize, we not lose sight of the particular. In fact, the ability to move back and forth between the specific and the general reveals more about both. As we will see, it is our relationship to the details that has the greater effect on our lives. Indeed, when we notice individual details, new ideas for generalizations can be drawn. We'd have more experiences that are as rich as Proust's recollection of the smell of madeleines. Just as Einstein imagined himself as a photon moving at the speed of light, *to draw a tree, we shouldn't just imagine touching a tree, we ought imagine being a tree.*

But to do so, we first have to really look at a tree.

Similitude in Dissimilitude

*I long ago came to the conclusion that even if I could put down accurately
the thing I saw and enjoyed, it would not give the observer the kind of
feeling it gave me. I had to create an equivalent for what I felt about
what I was looking at—not copy it.*
GEORGIA O'KEEFFE

Georgia O'Keeffe painted flowers so large that they could not be
overlooked even by those taught not to see. Perhaps the artist
knows instinctively that the map is not the territory and that
changing various aspects of the map may lead us to observe different things when we do experience the territory. When we realize that the name of something is not the same as the thing
named, we are able to see it more clearly. The possibility of new
metaphors may occur to us, and that possibility in turn can
teach us more about the individual case. How is it like a bird, a
bed, a restaurant?

William Wordsworth wrote appreciatively of "the pleasure
which the mind derives from the perception of similitude in
dissimilitude." But when we look at a forest, what do we see?
Often we do not see individual trees. Instead we see the common properties of trees. Seeing the individual tree and seeing
the forest are quite different, but the difference is qualitative
and not quantitative. What we have learned to look for determines mostly what we see in our lives. Imagine being asked to
look at a painting filled with birds, dogs, and cats and determining whether it contains more two-legged or four-legged
creatures. Although it's fine to appreciate the painting without
absorbing details like the number of cats it contains, were we
then asked whether there were more cats or dogs in it, we would
probably need to check the painting again.

In a demonstration that I conduct often, I ask the students in my classes whether I have time to tell them a story before going on to the lesson at hand. They look at their watches and say, "Yes, there is enough time." I then ask them what time it is, and to a one, they look at their watches once more. Shouldn't they know what time it is, given that they just looked at their watches? No, they shouldn't. In the first instance, they weren't really looking at what time it was, they were looking for the answer to the question about enough time, not *the* time. It is not surprising that they didn't know the exact time. If we look for one thing, we may easily miss another. Thus, while our expectations help us see, they also blind us to what we don't expect. But we can exert more control over what we see by changing our expectations.

To stay with watches a moment longer, compare an analog watch and a digital watch. The latter tells us most clearly what the precise time is, for its very display is the current time. Of course, there is no way of telling whether it is the correct time, and the current time is the only information it offers. But an analog watch tells us time in context, the "almost," "just past," and "soon it will be" times in addition to the current time. In some ways, this watch gives us more conditional information. Conditional information leads us to be more mindful, and when we are mindful, we see more.

Look at the fifteen coins on the next page and pick out the one that looks most like a penny. When Raymond Nickerson and M. J. Adams asked subjects to do so, they found that, in general, people don't know which is the accurate rendering of a penny, despite how familiar a penny is to most of us.[1] We can't identify it from the set of similar others because the differences that would help us in this task are irrelevant to the way we use pennies. A blue penny, for instance, would be easily noticed because when we reach for change we have to discriminate between, say a dime and a penny, and color helps us to do so. If

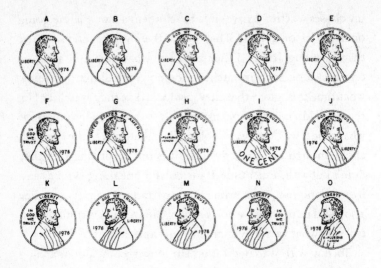

you collected coins, especially pennies, you would surely notice details about them that most of us ignore. Do the rest of us save time by never looking at the coin?

Looking but Not Seeing

Art is not what you see, but what you make others see.
EDGAR DEGAS

Researchers Dan Simons and Dan Levin conducted a wonderful study that demonstrates our mindlessness and just how much we fail to see in our everyday lives.[2] The experimenter randomly stops fellow pedestrians to ask for directions. As they talk, two confederates carrying a door walk between them and, unbeknownst to the participant, one of the people carrying the door changes places with the person asking for directions. The new person continues the conversation with the pedestrian, receiving the directions that were requested, and goes along his way. When questioned later, only 50 percent of the subjects realized that they were giving directions to two different people. Should they have realized it? They looked right at the person but didn't really see him. The individual aspects of that person, however, weren't very relevant to responding to the request for directions. The subject was focused on helping a stranger, whose identity was unimportant. Would it have taken much time to notice the particular individual? I think not, but at the least we should be aware that looking and seeing are different things.

Look at this drawing. Some people see a single figure, others see both an old woman and a young woman. To recognize the young woman, look for her beret, she's facing to the right. The neck of the young woman may also be seen as the nose of an old woman. You may have seen this sort of picture before. If so, your certainty about the dual nature of the image probably led you to look at it, recognize that there was more than one figure, and turn away with a haughty satisfaction. If this description

fits, you now have the opportunity to recognize everyday mindlessness. If you look again, this time with uncertainty, you may come to see yet a third person in the picture. The collar for both women is the mustache of a man.

Look at the illustration of a man. Even though now you'll probably look more carefully, it is difficult to see that there is more than one figure depicted here. It's harder because the previous exercise has led us to learn mindlessly that the *whole* fig-

ure may be seen in different ways. Our mind-sets are so strong that we set ourselves up to approach this new exercise with the same expectations, thinking we now know how to look at pictures. In this case, however, the second figure is a *part* of the whole (look carefully at the end of his nose).

Consider again a study conducted by the psychologists Jerome Bruner and Mary Potter in the 1960s, for it makes an important point about how our unease with uncertainty gets in the way of what we see.[3] They asked participants to identify a series of images they displayed. Initially, each image was far too blurry to be recognizable, but the experimenter could slowly bring them into focus, step-by-step. The image stayed blurry for one group longer than for the other. Then, for both groups, the image slowly came into view. The group for whom the image was blurry longer had trouble identifying it when it finally came into view. Being uncomfortable with uncertainty, they had labeled it prematurely, and now they couldn't easily relabel it.

When we travel, we expect to see things that are new. For many of us this desire is the very reason we get on an airplane.

We are typically more mindful when we travel, without any effort or intention to be so. As a result, we often pay closer attention and see more than when we are home. For example, when in Florence, I take note of the architecture of the many churches. In New York, I may barely notice the buildings. Once when I was in Israel I visited the ancient citadel Masada, and I picked up an unusually shaped rock to take home as a souvenir. I must have done so with the kind of confidence that leads others to be convinced it is the thing to do. Another woman, seeing me collect my prize, picked up a rock for herself and then asked her companions, "Do you have any idea how old this rock is?" I'll venture to say that she probably doesn't ask herself such questions back home, where the rocks, of course, aren't any younger.

There is no convincing reason to believe that our blindness affects us in only mundane ways. Consider the physician, for example, who has to read mammograms or other types of X-rays. If our mindless expectations govern what we see, then it may be the case that even our most experienced doctors can miss what is in plain view—what may be seen by the somewhat less experienced physician whose confidence has not yet eradicated his uncertainty. We are currently testing this hypothesis.

The More We Know the More Blind We Become

The most beautiful thing we can experience is the mysterious.
ALBERT EINSTEIN

Only when he no longer knows what he is doing
does the painter do good things.
EDGAR DEGAS

Most people think it is in their best interest to learn things so well that they become second nature to us. But is that true? We have all learned that stop signs are red and octagonal, and we slow our cars automatically when we see one, without really reading what a particular sign might actually say. Would it take significantly longer to make sure we read it? What are the costs when we don't?

The psychologist Elizabeth Loftus has conducted a number of important studies that demonstrate how susceptible we are as a result of our everyday blindness.[4] In one of them, participants were shown a videotape of an automobile accident that took place at a typical stop sign. Experimenters then asked them a series of leading questions about the accident that referred to the events having taken place at "the yield sign." When they were later asked to recount the accident, participants placed the accident at a yield sign.

The ramifications of this finding for eyewitnesses in court cases are important. There is now a good deal of research that shows how poor eyewitness accuracy is. In fact, the confidence people feel when they look and can identify what they see is the very thing that prevents witnesses from seeing what is otherwise in plain view. An interesting finding in this work is that confidence and accuracy are not correlated. That is, people may be absolutely sure of what they have seen, and they may be wrong.

The Greek philosopher Empedocles offered a theory of vision which maintained that sight arises from an active relationship between the seer and the seen. Perhaps the Greeks saw more than we typically do. Why didn't we learn from them? The Indian shamans of Peru, Buddhists, Sufis, and others may also have a better phenomenological understanding of what sight means than most of us do. Things started to run amok for us as we moved toward a rationalist view, in which we see the objective world existing independent of ourselves. Seeing is typically a passive process for us. The movement toward objectivity began with Plato's dichotomy between pure thought and material reality. In the 1400s, the Black Plague left people frightened of uncertainty. Science was to rescue us and remove that uncertainty, but in doing so it may have blinded us to sensuous knowledge. I am a scientist, so of course, I am not decrying science or suggesting science has done more harm than good. Instead, I am suggesting that there is a way to treat the "people-created objective" so that we don't lose sight.

With the rise of science, possibilities gave way to probabilities. As we search for the "right" answer, the potential opportunities that result from many alternatives and the vagaries of our intuition are problems to be ignored or held constant. We learn early on to break up experience into units—activities have beginnings and ends, days have minutes and hours, and so on. In her book *Sight and Sensibility: The Ecopsychology of Perception,* Laura Sewall maintains that these "broken experiences are unnatural and fundamentally discontinuous." They help create the illusion of separation between us and nature.

Yet, with a little thought, we could realize that what we see is dependent on relationships and not on discrete units. Figure-ground relationships or the context in which the target appears allows us to see it. It is the relationship between the signals from more than one receptor—one thing in relation to another—that leads us to see. According to Sewall, the edges *between* things—between the mountains and the sky, the sea and the shore—are of paramount importance. The edge marks both the figure and the ground. It is these edges that we become aware of when we decide to paint or take a photograph.

One way to start seeing, according to Sewall, is to attend to the spaces *in between,* in other words, the negative space. If we do so, Sewall says our attention will naturally widen and we will see more deeply into things. The primary function of our imagination is to bridge this negative space and close the gap between dualities. This is what makes things seem seamlessly real. Seeing, by contrast, could, and perhaps should, be an active process. In my view, we've become so adept at mindlessly naming things, forgetting that the "name" and the "named" are not the same, that perceiving the external world seems effortless. But in this adeptness, we rob ourselves of what could be seen if we only looked more mindfully.

Sewall tells of an exercise she uses in teaching vision improvement. She spills onto a table some kitchen utensils, scissors, matches, a can opener, batteries, and tape, and asks students to close their eyes and visualize a pair of scissors. Once the image is clearly formed in their minds, she tells them to open their eyes and try to find the can opener. It takes them much longer to do so than it does for those asked to search for the scissors. Imagining something makes it easier to see, and seeing that object repeatedly makes it easier to imagine. The neural networks subserving a particular image are strengthened each time we see or imagine it, and each time the world we see becomes more integrated and seemingly less a function of how we perceive it. The easier it becomes to see the world we expect to see, the harder it becomes to see the unexpected.

Imagining something, however, may make it easier to see only if there is a strong physical relationship between the imagined and the seen. Consider, for example, the not infrequent occurrence of looking for something we expect to find that is right where we are looking, but still we fail to see it. I was looking for a large painting I did on Masonite board that I couldn't seem to find anywhere. As I searched, I tried hard to imagine the painting, thinking that doing so would help. It turned out this may have been the very thing that prevented me from seeing it. The painting was facing the wall. Later, when a friend had found it for me, I was surprised at how wrong I had been all along about the size of the painting. I was looking for a much larger painting, and so I didn't see it. Let's imagine that I'm looking for my wallet. If my memory of the wallet is not exactly as the wallet looks now (that is, if it's sitting at a different orientation, the light is different, et cetera), sharpening my old image of what I thought it looked like should make it harder to find.

If we learn something mindfully, we essentially enshroud it in some uncertainty, and this uncertainty is what allows us to see. Psychologists have found that some of us are better at "finding the hidden object" than others. Typically males are more field independent than females are, and females are typically field dependent. *Field independence* is an ability to separate figure from ground; field dependence is an inability to separate figure from ground. I see this concept very differently. Years ago, Benzion Chanowitz and I were preparing stimulus materials for a study we were designing. We counted the hidden objects in a picture from a children's magazine. There was a fish on a child's pants leg. Benzion saw it as a hidden figure. But I saw it as a design on the pants. That difference gave rise to the idea that perhaps females like me were field sensitive, able to integrate figure and ground. That would make males like Benzion field insensitive, unable to integrate figure and ground. Thus, while field dependence seems bad, field integration seems good. The more mindful one is, the better one should be at integrating when integrating is desired and being field independent when that is desired. That is, mindfulness provides us with choices.

Right now most of us see what we expect to see without realizing that there is a choice. In an experiment designed by psychologist Dan Simons, participants were shown a videotape of a basketball game and asked to count the number of passes made by one of the teams. In the middle of the game, a person dressed in a gorilla suit quite clearly walks onto the court, stops, and beats his chest. No one could have missed that, you would think. Well, approximately half of the participants did not see him. When asked if they had noticed anything unusual during the game, they reported that they had not. When told of the gorilla, they were surprised and had to be shown the tape again.

While discussing the experiment in our lab, we noticed that many of us saw the gorilla when we first viewed the tape. Was it because we were more mindful than others? Kevin Williams and I recently showed the videotape to my class to see whether mindful observers were more likely to notice the gorilla. Before we showed the tape, we randomly handed out two sets of written instructions. Half of the participants received instructions that were the same as those Dan gave his research participants, to "count the number of passes that are made." The other half were given instructions on being mindful. We explained that each basketball game is similar to all others in some ways, which is why we call them by the same name, but also that each is different in some ways from any other game they may have seen. We asked the participants to notice the ways this game of basketball was both similar to and different from the last basketball game they saw. Most of those who were instructed to be mindful noticed the gorilla, while those who counted passes did not.

Finding Perspective and Gaining Control

In the end, she will manage to look just like it.
PABLO PICASSO, upon being told that his portrait of
Gertrude Stein looked nothing like her

Imagine we are sitting across a table from each other. If I ask you to envision the scene from my perspective, you are likely to look directly at me in an attempt to do so. Of course, you aren't really gaining my perspective at all; what I see from my perspective is you. For many beginning artists (and even writers, in a sense) the most frustrating aspect of early efforts is getting the perspective right. But whose perspective do we mean?

I once invited my friend the artist Barbara Cohen over to see a painting I had just finished. It was an early painting on a canvas measuring about three feet by four feet. I had depicted a woman sitting at a table, working on her computer, with another woman standing supportively behind her, looking over her shoulder. There are canvases strewn about and dogs resting in several places. There was also a couch in the room. A sweet smile came over Barbara's face as she studied the couch. I asked what she found amusing. She said she'd tell me if I promised not to change anything in the painting. I wouldn't agree, but I convinced her to tell me anyway. She pointed out that the couch was on its back with the legs pointed into the room. I was aghast. How could I have been so blind, I thought. As soon as she had left, I quickly "moved" the furniture in the painting, which turned out to be a good deal harder than if the couch had actually been on its back in my living room.

I had looked at the original painting many times but saw no problem with it. Why hadn't I noticed this obvious thing? Late that night, it struck me. I might have been new to painting, but I had been looking at things all my life. Why did I paint the room that way? I looked again at the painting and realized that I had painted the couch from the perspective of the people in the painting. It was they, after all, who would use the couch. Why hadn't I first seen it from Barbara's perspective? Just as interesting, one might counter, why didn't she see it from mine? If either I or Barbara had been aware of the perspective from which I was painting, it would have made sense. In fact, as I looked at the painting again, I saw that the odd perspective had been one of its more interesting aspects. It still troubles me that I so easily become blinded to my own perspective and adopt someone else's ideas.

To know that our work can be more engaging precisely because we don't have it quite right is liberating. Barbara still claims that I have furniture dyslexia, and that would seem to be true in at least one sense. I often paint furniture from my mind's inner perspective, and it can be quite cockeyed when I look at the finished painting from a new perspective. In fact, I've learned often to vary the perspective as I paint, which can make things very interesting indeed. And so, I have rejected her use of the word *dyslexia* and choose to see what I paint as simply my vision of furniture. Indeed, it may be this very "problem" that makes some of the work more interesting. Soon, I might even stop using the rather mindless word *cockeyed* to describe these paintings.

Armed with the awareness of how different things look depending on perspective, we open up many more choices for ourselves. Change the perspective and we have a new painting.

Openness to different points of view is an important aspect of being mindfully creative. As already noted, social psychologists have long written about the differences between the perspective of an actor and that of an observer. Research has shown that we are likely to blame circumstances for our negative behavior: "The elevator always makes me late." If the very same behavior is engaged in by someone else, however, we tend to blame that individual: "He is chronically behind schedule."

Once we become mindfully aware of views other than our own, we start to realize that there are as many views as there are observers. Such awareness is potentially liberating. Imagine that someone has just told you that you are rude, but you thought you were being frank. If only one perspective can be correct, you can't both be right. But with an awareness that there are many legitimate perspectives, you could accept that you are both right and instead focus on whether your words had the effect you wanted to produce. When we cling to our own point of view, we may blind ourselves to our impact on others; if we are too vulnerable to other people's definitions of our behavior, we can feel undermined, for observers are typically less flattering of us than we are of ourselves. It is easy to see that any interaction between people can have *at least* two interpretations: spontaneous versus weak, intense versus emotional, and so on.

This is not meant to give the impression that for every act there are two set, polarized interpretations. As we said, there are potentially as many interpretations as there are observers. Every idea, person, or object is simultaneously many things depending on the perspective from which it is viewed. A steer may be steak to a rancher, a sacred object to a Hindu, and a collection of genes and proteins to a molecular biologist. Instead, we need to remain aware that the number of possible perspectives will never be exhausted.

The consequences of trying out different perspectives are important. First, we gain more choice in how to respond. A single-minded label produces an automatic reaction, which reduces our options. Also, to understand that other people may not be so different allows us empathy and enlarges our range of responses. We are less likely to feel locked into a polarized struggle.

Second, when we apply this open-minded attitude to our own behavior, change becomes more possible. When I used to do clinical work, it seemed odd to me that not only did many people in therapy have strong motivation to change (hence their visits to me) but the desired behavior was already in their repertoires. What was stopping them? In looking back, I realize that they were probably trying to change behavior (for example, "being impulsive") they actively enjoyed but from another point of view ("being spontaneous"). With this realization, changing one's behavior might be seen not as changing something negative but as making a choice between two positive alternatives (for example, "being reflective" versus "being spontaneous").

If seeing depends in large part on believing, then how can we learn to see more? We have already seen and learned much about the world. How can we learn to see it all again? Part of the answer, from my perspective, was suggested in each preceding chapter of this book. By recognizing that evaluation is not stable and independent of context, for example, or by putting people back in the equation, we should increase our uncertainty. It is in this uncertainty that we have the possibility of creating new options for ourselves.

Any new activity we undertake has the potential to reveal to us that which we don't know. The uncertainty before us will serve us well as long as we make a universal, rather than a personal, attribution for it. That is, uncertainty is the rule for all of us, not just for the individual. If I don't know but think "it" is knowable, i.e., certain, then I feel insecure and am afraid to go forward. When I realize that I don't know but neither does anyone else, I am less afraid. Stability is a mind-set, and those with unbridled confidence that they are right confuse the stability of their mind-sets with the stability of the underlying phenomena. Confidence and certainty are not the same.

Painting, writing, learning to play an instrument, or any other new activity provokes mindfulness and reveals much of what was hidden for us. In the past I would have described trees as green. Now I see a multitude of colors when I look at trees, even when I just think about them. I now know that I don't know what any particular tree will look like without first seeing it, and even then it is likely to be more than I see.

Do artists paint what they see, what they know, or what they imagine? If we view any painting from a single perspective, we think if the artist doesn't paint what we see she must have worked from imagination. Wouldn't it be interesting to consider that what we are looking at is what the artist actually saw? For example, to consider pre-Columbian art to be realistic rather than symbolic. What's more, if I pretend I am the thing I want to draw or paint, I may see it better. If I reduce its size or make it much larger, that which stays constant can reveal to me what I take to be important.

If I paint a portrait, I'm painting what feels to me like the essence of the person. If I take the time to give the nose and other facial features depth, the emotion often fades for me. I didn't realize this until I was able to paint a nose so that it did indeed look the way a nose is "supposed" to look. I'm not interested in painting noses very often, however. I usually want to paint a portrait wherein the individual parts are less than the whole. When we look at the work of self-taught artists or untrained artists, we should be careful not to think that the choices they made were made by default, because of limited possibility of expression.

Can you draw a reasonably straight line? A curved line? A thick, bold line or curve? A thin line or curve? Can you recognize different colors? If so, all that is left to be able to draw or paint is to learn how to see. To play an instrument, all you need to learn is to hear. It is that simple.

9

From Reference to Preference

The face of the water, in time, became a wonderful book—a book that was a dead language to the uneducated passenger, but which told its mind to me without reserve, delivering its most cherished secrets as clearly as if it uttered them with a voice.
MARK TWAIN, *Life on the Mississippi*

MY FRIEND AND COLLEAGUE DUNCAN LUCE AND I LEFT OUR offices one day to take a look at Harvard's then-new Sackler Museum. All of the exhibitions had not yet been installed, and on the wall opposite the entrance white curtains covered what soon would be a new installation of paintings. As we stood there deciding where to go first, a couple entered the museum, studied the curtains carefully, and proceeded to wax eloquent on the "art" they saw before them. When they were out of earshot, Duncan and I shared our amusement at their mistake. In hindsight, however, I think the joke was on us. That couple clearly enjoyed looking at the curtains; we had barely considered them. They mindfully engaged the curtains and created a work of art for themselves, which they enjoyed greatly. Our educated mind-sets meant that all we could see was a wall of uninteresting curtains.

As we've been seeing from one perspective or another throughout this book, we all exhibit a strong tendency to mindlessly take the world as it is given to us, and in so doing, we give up much more control than we realize. We passively wait for something out there to grab our attention, something about which we can feel some passion and with which we can engage. As a result, we tend not to reach out to new things, which are more difficult to connect to because we don't know them as well.

We can, however, learn to choose our passions actively, to become mindfully attentive to them and totally involved in them. In such complete engagement lies a real benefit of mindfulness—we become attracted to that with which we engage. Whether it is a painting or even our own appearance, mindful exposure to something increases our enjoyment of it. In essence, the more we see it mindfully, the more we like it.

We've already seen how blind we can be to much of the world. Actively noticing new things opens our eyes to more than that which takes our immediate attention. We've transformed ourselves from someone like Truman Capote's character P. B. Jones—who describes perhaps the most exciting city in the world, Paris, as mere scenery—to someone like Gertrude Stein—for whom seeing Jean-François Millet's painting *The Man with the Hoe* made France "ground not country."[1]

To actively engage the world means to see more, remember more of what we've seen, and most important, like that which we now see all the more. For years I have conducted a demonstration in my large lecture class on social psychology. I select a male volunteer from the students and ask him to stand up so that everyone can look at him. Of course, the student is a bit embarrassed, but over the years they all have endured the ordeal. I then ask the student to leave the room for a moment. When he has left, I unveil three large posters, each of a beautiful young woman, and ask the class to vote for the woman the student most resembles. When a consensus has been reached, the volunteer is brought back into the lecture hall and asked to look at the three women and tell us which one he finds most attractive. To this day, the student has always chosen the woman the class decided he most resembles.

Earlier, I wrote that mindful creativity can turn lives troubled by boredom and loneliness into lives that are rich and exciting. A rich, creative life really is available to each of us, but only when we stop handing over control of our creative lives to the prejudices that tell us it is not available. To do so, we need to learn why it's important to reach out and embrace the world, to look at it with a fresh perspective and an eye to what is new and distinct about it. In the process, we don't just gain a more interesting, more likable approach to the world but have the chance to relieve ourselves of some of the pain we too often cause ourselves. In this chapter, I want to explore how creative engagement can make us like ourselves and others better, improving our overall happiness and even our health.

Discovering to Enjoy

I can't understand why people are frightened of new ideas.
I'm frightened of the old ones.
JOHN CAGE

In 1979, while I was living in San Francisco for the year, a lawyer came to see me to discuss a business venture. He was a nice man, but I must admit that I found him physically very unattractive right from the start. We worked on the project for several hours, until a horn honked outside, announcing that his ride home had arrived. Looking out the window, I saw two beautiful women in a sporty, red convertible waving enthusiastically to him. I remember my surprise when I looked back at him, now noting more of his features, and saw someone I found quite attractive. The lesson has always stayed with me. When we learn to see things with a new perspective and engage them mindfully, our experience can be quite different than we would imagine.

Consider the attention we usually give to ourselves and what that means. We look at ourselves in the mirror every day, and every day we notice some new small things that we didn't notice the time before. A friend of mine has an Afro. When she combs her hair, it looks no different to me than before she did so, but to her there is a distinct difference. We look at ourselves over and over again, and most of us basically like what we see, save perhaps a few pounds too many or muscles too few. It may not be obvious, but the fact that we mindfully pay attention to ourselves leads us basically to like what we see much more than we realize.

Our lab has conducted a number of experiments to test the idea that drawing novel distinctions increases liking. In one study, we played a tape of rap music to people we had recruited who claimed that they didn't like rap and a tape of classical music for those who said they didn't like classical. We asked some of each of them to note three new things about the music as they listened, and we had others notice six new things. A third, control, group wasn't asked to make any new distinctions about the music they were listening to.

We found that, despite their initial dislike of the music, the more new things participants noticed about it, the more they told us they liked it. In a related experiment, we asked women who told us they thought football was boring to watch a tape of the Super Bowl, having some of them draw novel distinctions about the game. Once again, the group asked to noticed new things told us that they liked the game more than did those who were not asked to draw distinctions. The group asked to draw the most distinctions enjoyed the game the most. Whether it was in finding new meanings in the lyrics, picking out individual instruments from an orchestra, or recognizing the rear ends of football players, the findings strongly supported the hypothesis that noticing new things increases our liking of them.

In research Andrea Marcus and I conducted, we sought to see how strongly active engagement with unfamiliar paintings could affect our preferences for them.[2] We asked subjects to look at a painting that they had never before seen, assigning some the task of noticing novel aspects of the work while giving others no such instructions. We then showed them a second painting and asked both groups to compare it with the first. As soon as they had finished their assignment, we asked them all to sign their names on a clipboard to indicate the painting they liked more. The clipboard held a sheet of paper with the title of each painting across the top. Under one title we had written a single signature, under the other a list of signatures that seemed to indicate the strong preference of previous participants for that painting. Usually, we would expect that subjects would be influenced by the relative sizes of the lists, but we wondered whether those subjects who were asked to draw mindful distinctions would feel strongly enough about their preferences to go against the judgment of other participants. In fact, they did. These participants were also more confident of their feelings than were the subjects who had been asked merely to judge the paintings.

A student in my class, Steven Long, recently conducted a similar study involving people's preference for different brands of chocolate.[3] It is well-known that there are strong brand preferences for chocolate, and the study was designed to investigate whether a mindful approach would affect that preference. Participants were given samples of a little inexpensive chocolate or an expensive chocolate (Godiva), in their original wrappings or boxed as the other. One group was asked to draw five novel distinctions about the chocolate by completing sentences such as "This chocolate reminds me of . . ." or "This chocolate's texture is similar to . . . ," and one group was not. Finally, all were asked to rate their samples. The chocolates for which participants drew distinctions were rated higher, regardless of whether they were the expensive or the inexpensive brand.

In each of these studies, it became clear that taking notice of things expands our appreciation of them. These findings constitute a powerful argument for taking on creative endeavors. Our own creative engagement is able to help us learn to appreciate and like the world around us in much the same fashion. Just how strong is this effect, and is it limited to music, football, chocolates, and paintings?

Seeing Each Other Differently

No surprise for the writer, no surprise for the reader.
ROBERT FROST

People naturally seek novelty, but when what psychologists call the "novel stimulus" is a person, we are presented with a powerful cultural roadblock—we are taught not to look too closely at others. And if we can't look, we find it easier to avoid the person than to deal with the conflict between wanting to look and the cultural norms preventing our looking. Colleagues Shelley Taylor, Susan Fiske, Benzion Chanowitz, and I proposed this hypothesis many years ago and tested it by inviting one of our experimental groups to view a handicapped or pregnant person alone in a room (the novel stimulus) through a one-way mirror before they interacted with that person.[4] The experiments showed that the opportunity to mindfully notice many new things about the target person indeed resulted in increased engagement when they later met the person.

Expanding on those findings, work psychologist Lois Imber and I conducted suggests how important it is that we mindfully engage people.[5] When we notice someone acting differently from what we expect and do not engage in further mindful distinction drawing, we end up making very extreme evaluations of that person. Worse still, if we then notice even a few little things about the person that we don't typically notice in most people—not because they aren't there but rather because we are typically mindless to their presence—we conclude that the person may be even more different than we first thought. This is, in fact, a basis for our discrimination against others: that our failure to see them fully leads us to exaggerate and deal harshly with the obvious differences between us and them.

Our lab wanted to see whether increased mindfulness would decrease discrimination. Richard Bashner, Benzion Chanowitz, and I devised a study in which we showed children slides of people with disabilities and asked questions about them.[6] Some children were asked to provide only one answer to the questions, others several answers to each question. For example, they were shown a slide of a woman they were told was deaf. Some children were asked to name one way she might be good at her job as cook. Others were asked to name four ways she might be good at her job and four ways she might be bad at it.

Next, the children were told that a child with a disability was coming to their school. They were asked if they wanted to attend a picnic with that child or have that child as a partner for various activities. Children who had been asked to provide multiple answers to our questions about the people in the slides were less likely to want to avoid the new child, and their responses were more differentiated. For example, they were more likely to want a blind child as a partner in an activity for which blindness could be an advantage, such as pin-the-tail-on-the-donkey, but not for an activity for which they thought blindness could be a disadvantage, such as a wheelchair race.

This research suggests that we should actively make more distinctions among people, rather than follow the proverbial wisdom which tells us we should see ourselves and one another as alike. We are alike in that we are all very different from one another. Not only can doing so increase our liking for others but it breaks down traditional in-group and out-group distinctions. An experiment lab members Sarit Golub, Megan Kozak, and I just completed tested most strongly the effect of mindful distinction drawing and the reduction of prejudice.[7] We wanted to see if we could use this technique to decrease prejudice against homosexuals and people with AIDS. We told subjects that they would be participating in a series of studies on their perception of others, field perception, and political attitudes at Harvard. All were told they were first to watch a brief video and then to follow the instructions in a package we left with them. Some of the subjects were told to watch the video carefully, noticing as many things as possible about the person in it, a young man named John. Others were also told to note carefully as much as possible about a person in a different video, a young gay man. Two control groups were told to watch their videos without any instructions to note things about its subject, and they were not informed whether he was gay or not.

Afterward, all subjects were asked to evaluate the person in the video based on a list of words that described a range of characteristics, such as intelligent, likable, unreliable, composed, flamboyant, or sensitive. The list was constructed to offer words that evoke positive, negative, neutral, or stereotypical assessments of people. In addition, the subjects were asked to complete a questionnaire about their political views, designed to elicit their attitudes about gay rights. Asking subjects to make mindful distinctions about people tended to mitigate their negative assessments of them in particular and more generally about the stereotype.

Mindfully drawing new distinctions, thus, helps us come to know and like others. The strategy also works well on people we thought we knew already. Often we notice much about a new romantic partner, and because of all we notice, we begin to feel passion for him or her. But then we let the newness wear off and stability takes over.[8] That is, at some point we stop noticing the people we have cared about most. Well, not quite. We don't do this for our children or even for our plants. We expect them to change, we look for differences, and we come to care more and more.

The Genius of Engagement

The best reason to paint is that there is no reason to paint. . . . I'd like to pretend that I've never seen anything, never read anything, never heard anything . . . and then make something. . . . Every time I make something I think about the people who are going to see it and every time I see something, I think about the person who made it. . . . Nothing is important . . . so everything is important.
KEITH HARING

In the late 1960s, Philip Goldberg conducted a study in which participants read an essay identified as written by either Joan McKay or John McKay.[9] Although the two essays were exactly the same, participants were more willing to engage and thus appreciate the essay they thought had been written by a man.

Goldberg was primarily interested in revealing gender prejudice, not in whether the name of the author provoked different
levels of engagement with the paper. If I were to replicate his
study today, I would especially want to note the effect of the author's gender on the amount of time spent reading the essay
and the participants' ability to remember its contents. We did
much the same thing in a recent experiment.

In an extension of a study discussed earlier, members of the
lab Wendy Smith, Adrienne Baker, Tal Ben-Schachar, and I
found that, with a little provocation, people can increase their
enjoyment of art no matter who the artist is.[10] We asked four
groups of participants to look at a painting we were reasonably
sure they wouldn't have seen before. The first group was shown
an obscure painting by Henri Matisse (and told that he was the
artist); the second group was shown a painting by an unknown
artist, whom we called Regnal. The other two groups, however,
were shown either a Matisse identified as a Regnal or a Regnal
identified as a Matisse. Given that all the paintings were obscure,
there was little chance that anyone would spot the misattribu-
tion. Once again we timed how long the participants spent with
the painting and took various measures of how much they liked
it. We decided to use two different paintings of mine and Matisse to make sure that we were studying the effect of painter status and not just a particular painting. Not surprisingly, when
the artist was identified as Matisse, participants liked the painting better than when Regnal was said to be the artist, no matter
who in fact had painted it. When the artist was identified as Regnal even though it was actually Matisse, people spent little time
looking at the painting and reported that they didn't like it very
much. The Matisse painting wasn't his best, but to my surprise,
when the Regnal paintings were said to be by Matisse, they were
actually preferred to those in fact painted by Matisse!

When my collaborators suggested that we use my paintings, I was very hesitant. I wasn't eager, to be honest, to have others judge my work alongside that of Matisse. But they reminded me of my work on evaluation and prevailed. Besides, they argued, if my paintings really had no merit, they would provide a stronger test of our hypothesis.

Of course, this comparison should not be taken too seriously, despite how much fun it was for me. We should take seriously, however, the way we engage our world when we have external reason to do so. In my view, Matisse is clearly an artist with a well-deserved reputation. Not every painting of his, however, needs to be considered a masterpiece. Nevertheless, when a painting is said to be by Matisse, people are willing to engage it. When we engage something, we like it more and the experience is more rewarding for us. Both of these experiments show us that mindful engagement can be internally provoked and does not rely on any particular external stimulus. When the participants presumed the painting was by an unknown artist, they were unwilling to find it interesting. As a result, the experience was less enjoyable than it could have been.

When a work has been created by someone of status—an external factor—we typically take the time to engage it. But it is our degree of engagement, not the identity of the artist, that controls our enjoyment of the experience. The status of an artist is a useful indicator of what the culture finds approving. But why do we limit ourselves to that criterion? Our studies show that if we choose to engage whatever is before us, we are that much richer.

I recently read a charming book by Tracy Chevalier, *Girl with a Pearl Earring,* which was based on the author's interpretation of and creative engagement with the famous painting by the Dutch painter Jan Vermeer. Vermeer's portrait depicts a young girl sitting in a prosperous Dutch household. In the novel, the shy young heroine is a servant in the house. First Vermeer's assistant, she later becomes his model. The novel plays on domestic tensions and Vermeer's relationship with his jealous wife and guarded mother-in-law. All of this was, of course, completely invented, but descriptions of the heroine's daily life and humdrum duties reveal the mindfulness with which Chevalier had studied the painting:

> *I came to love grinding the things he brought from the apothecary—bones, white lead, madder, massicot—to see how bright and pure I could get the colors. I learned that the finer the materials were ground, the deeper the color. From rough, dull grains madder became a fine bright red powder and, mixed with linseed oil, a sparkling paint. Making it and the other colors was magical.*

Other examples of novels motivated by an engagement with art include Deborah Moggach's *Tulip Fever* and Susan Vreeland's *Girl in Hyacinth Blue*. We need not go as far as to write a novel ourselves, but surely if others are able, we can read enough into a painting to make it equally alive for us as we view it in a museum. And we needn't limit ourselves to museums. Just as the opening quotation of this chapter suggests, water—for Twain, the water of the Mississippi—can be a fascinating beginning. And, as suggested by Gertrude Stein, a place—for her, France—can be more than just a place.

The Mere Exposure of Creativity

Anything one does every day is important and imposing and anywhere one lives is interesting and beautiful.
GERTRUDE STEIN

All the research we've looked at thus far tells us that rather than breeding contempt, familiarity breeds liking. But too often the familiar becomes background that we mindlessly overlook. For

Gertrude Stein, such a life was impossible; perhaps it was living in France. The French seem to take great delight in attending to detail, and it is hard not to notice small distinctions when a people raise the commonplace to an art. The displays in every shop, the food in every restaurant, and of course, the fashion, all tell us the details matter. And with attention to (more accurately, the creation of) details, there comes a pride and personal touch that lead many an American to Paris, keeping themselves blind to the possibilities for mindful, creative living back home.

There is a very robust finding in social psychology called the "mere exposure effect." In study after study, researchers find that familiarity breeds liking—seeing something over and over again increases our liking for it. In one of the earliest studies on the topic, eminent psychologist Robert Zajonc had research participants read a list of unfamiliar Turkish words in which the number of times a particular word appeared varied. After hearing the list, participants were asked to make up definitions for these words. Zajonc found that the more frequently the word had appeared, the more positive the definition it was given. Repeated exposure provides more opportunity for mindful distinction drawing. Once we think we know something, we usually cease to pay much attention to it, and the effect of repeated exposure wears off unless we continue to be mindful.

The more distinctions we draw, the more we see into the essence of something. Think about it. We find, for instance, rich, detailed writing evocative. The masterpieces of literature—say those of Shakespeare or Homer—contain detail that is able to resonate across geographic boundary and time. The same is true for art. Whether or not we like the painting, the *Mona Lisa*, for example, presents us with an enigmatic smile that, while explicit and detailed, is ultimately ambiguous. It was ambiguous when Leonardo da Vinci first painted it, it is ambiguous now, and it seems, it probably will be ambiguous a century from now. Its ambiguity is its essence.

If it is the mindful engagement with the world that leads us to enjoy the world, when we don't seek this mindful engagement, the consequences may be more than just the absence of enjoyment. They may be painful. Much of the time, as we wait for something to grab us, something comes along. But we all know what it feels like when the waiting is painfully long and we feel empty without realizing why.

Often when students finish their dissertations, they experience a letdown. Their work required putting everything else aside, giving full attention to the matter at hand, and leaving it behind causes the emptiness they feel when it's over. But we rarely understand these experiences in straightforward ways. Instead, we turn the emptiness to feeling bad about ourselves or to seeking out grand, existential reasons for the emptiness we feel. The end of a relationship breeds similar feelings of emptiness. Here most of us come to believe that another person is required for us to feel engaged, but too often we believe no one but the person who left can fit the bill. And so we feel we aren't in control of the situation; we can't return to writing a dissertation that we've finished; and we often can't (or don't really want to) return to our old relationship. But this feeling of helplessness may be wrongheaded. Most control comes from our realizing that there are multiple sources of engagement—that whatever we choose to engage, we can engage. But to do so, we need to understand how to change our perception of the situation.

Language has the interesting property of being able to increase and decrease our perceptions of control. We aren't very aware of how language limits our control. Linguists know that language works through metaphor and that different metaphors can direct our thoughts about a single situation in many ways, as different as the number of metaphors considered. We typically accept single understandings or descriptions for our feelings that limit the very experiences they describe.

All that we've been discussing has importance far beyond art for art's sake. Indeed, the larger message is art for life's sake. We accept single labels for even life-threatening events when doing so may have dramatic consequences. Consider for a moment how we regard the victory over our last cold. While there are surely similarities among the numerous colds we have had over the course of our lifetimes, there are also many differences. The more distinctions we draw, the easier it is for us to know how to respond to each type of cold, and many of us do just that, treating each cold as something unique and attending to each in its own way. Each cold is similar to each other cold, and each is also different. No one decided whether we attend to the similarities or to the differences. Most of us are oblivious to the idea that there was any choice involved. We see each cold as different. We believe we can beat the new cold because we've beaten many of them in the past.

In contrast to the way we deal with colds, think about the way we deal with cancer. If somebody is diagnosed as having cancer and then the cancer goes away, we say he is in remission. The implication of that word is that the cancer may well recur, and if it does it will be the same cancer. Surely if cancer recurs it will in some ways bear a similarity to the last cancer, but in some ways it just as surely will be different. Our language leads us to see the similarity in each instance of cancer, while with the common cold we looked for dissimilarities, if we looked at all. In 1979, at age fifty-six, my mother died of breast cancer. That's what the medical world reported. But I'm still not sure. Because before she died, her cancer went into a complete "remission." If two people go for a checkup to see if they have cancer and one never had the disease and the other is in "remission," the test results look the same. Should we call it remission or cure?

What difference does this difference make? It makes all the difference in the world. Each time we beat a common cold, we become more persuaded that we can beat the next one. With cancer, we can't feel that we've successfully conquered it because the medical world has told us that "it" may return. If it does return, it is seen as the same cancer. Psychologically, this belief leads us to feel defeated. In the case of a cold, "I did it before, I can do it again." For cancer, "I get weaker and weaker each time the cancer comes back and become more and more convinced that it is stronger than I am."

The psychological literature is now replete with examples of the physical consequences of giving up. People are more likely to die soon after the death of a spouse of many years, to die after rather than before holidays, and so on. Hard data make the same point. Even if one were not persuaded by these data, it is clear that giving up leads people not to do what would be good for them.[11] Why exercise or take medication if one is likely to soon die anyway? Did cancer kill my mother, or was she led to give up? The ability to see similarity or difference, to engage our lives mindfully, may be of great consequence.

The Terms of Engagement

It is only when I lose contact with the painting that the result is a mess.
Otherwise there is pure harmony, an easy give and take,
and the painting comes out well.
JACKSON POLLOCK

How is it that we come to engage ourselves with the world? First, we ought to understand the many beliefs we mindlessly hold disengage us from experience and result in unnecessary negative emotion.

One of the most powerful beliefs that keeps us from engaging mindfully with the world is the myth of endings. It appears at first to be quite innocuous, if not useful, and we all do it. In starting a task we impose on it a temporal structure and behave as if the task itself has a beginning, middle, and end. We do it for activities as wide-ranging as writing, exercising, having a baby, and even being in a relationship. We especially do it with creative activities. Consider a brief thought experiment to see the effects of this beginning-middle-end structure on tasks. When do you think you'd get tired if you were to do fifty jumping jacks? Most people I ask say after around thirty. But when asked, When do you think you'd get tired if you were to do seventy jumping jacks, most people I've asked say at around fifty. We can do thirty in the first case but fifty in the second. I believe this difference happens because we expect to get tired around two-thirds of the way through almost whatever we do.

The problem that arises from the myth of endings is that the structure controls our approach to the activity. It often takes a good deal of effort to "get into" a task, and knowing this, we seek to set an "end." We look at the structure we've created and seek to stop at what we believe is some natural end point. But there is no reason we have to stop there; we could stop anywhere. These "natural" breaks are, of course, completely artificial. When we reach the stopping point, we stop engaging, leaving us to start all over at a new "beginning" the next time. But if we instead left at some random time or in the "middle," we would know how to start the next time—we'd start just where we left off.

Packaging the world leads to disengagement. I'm finished eating a candy bar when there is no more left, that seems clear enough. If I broke it into five parts and realized each part was actually a whole—after all, who chose the initial size in the first place?—I could impose a different structure on what constitutes the beginning, middle, and end. Similarly, if someone cancels an appointment with me and I have an extra twenty minutes, how often do I get upset and "waste" the found time because it's not enough to do the things I need to do? Many of those "things" take long only because of the way we've structured them. If I broke them into a new set of parts, I could find many productive ways to spend that twenty minutes.

What we're doing is creating transitions for ourselves, and transitions are another form of disengagement. They are difficult for us because in transitions we are no longer engaged in what we are leaving and don't yet know enough about what we are approaching to engage it. There is a void. If we attribute our negative feelings to the move we are making, rather than the transition itself, we may think we made the wrong decision, and that brings its own set of problems. Waiting is a form of transition and thus another form of disengagement. If we didn't feel the last activity was over and the new one has not yet begun, we would not experience ourselves waiting to be engaged. When we come to a red light, we need to stop the car, not stop experiencing ourselves. There are interesting things to notice all around us if we think to look.

Each roadblock to our mindful creativity similarly inhibits our engagement. Consider evaluations. Early on we are taught to want that which we evaluate as good and avoid that which we decide is bad. Instead of having the experience with the target of the evaluation, we often use the evaluation alone as reason to approach or avoid and in so doing remove the reason for engagement. For example, when a painting is not by a known artist, we may overlook it. Indeed, we tend to avoid any person or thing that has been evaluated as negative and thus remove the opportunity to engage it. Even when the evaluation is positive, it may lead to mindless activity rather than engagement. Consider the "halo effect" in this regard. Learning that some artist, painting, or piece of music has been lavishly praised doesn't mean there aren't aspects of it that we might find less appealing than others. Similarly, consider the "pitchfork effect." When we or the culture have judged something negatively, that assessment doesn't mean that all parts of it are equally distasteful to us or that our judgment of it will be constant over time. Consider other examples of when positive evaluations may lead to mindlessness: I order what I know to be appealing in my favorite restaurant without consulting my current tastes; I buy a sweater because it is recommended and wear it without noticing the way it looks on me in various shades of light or with different apparel; I get a big (or a small) dog without considering how the other size might better suit my style of life now that I'm older.

Our fear of making mistakes, our belief that we have no talent, and our comparisons with others all keep us from engaging any creative activity, and they do so without our realizing that the terms of engagement are ours to impose. We need not passively wait for something to propel our motivation to engage.

Creative engagement does not require a new activity. Mindful engagement is a state of mind that we can actively initiate at any time. I often compare mindfulness to living in a transparent house. Everything in the house is there for us to perceive and to be available to us. When in the living room, we could still see an object in the attic even if we chose not to attend to it or use it that minute. If we were mindfully creative, we would be in this ever-ready state of mind at all times. Of course, we don't want to think of or make use of everything all the time, but all is always available to us. We always have options, and this gives us greater control. The feeling of control, in turn, encourages us to be more mindful. It might take some effort to *change* from a mindless mode to a mindfully engaged mode, to take the steps to overcome the roadblocks in our way. But to be alert and open to new perspectives and new information is not difficult. Mindfulness is itself not effortful. It is literally and figuratively enlivening.

To be mindfully engaged is the most natural, creative state we can be in.

10

The Mindful Choice

I don't know in advance what I am going to put on canvas any more than I decide beforehand what colors I am going to use.
PABLO PICASSO

IT'S TIME TO GET STARTED. NOW THAT WE UNDERSTAND THAT WE shouldn't worry about what others will think about our first painting, poem, or whatever it is we choose to do, that comparing ourselves with others is not in our best interest, that talent is not necessary, in short, that we are going to engage our creativity mindfully, it is time to go to the store and get whatever we need.

Once we are there, however, the simple task of getting ready often quickly becomes daunting. How do we decide what we need? Should we start small or jump in headfirst? How do we know what the right start is? In the face of such uncertainty, we perhaps ought to pay close attention to Picasso's words: if we are to proceed mindfully, perhaps we shouldn't be interested in knowing the answers to these questions in advance. We should just buy whatever colors appeal to us, whatever brushes we think interesting, and some surface on which to paint.

Getting started at anything is like buying our first microwave. As the economist Thomas Schelling is fond of saying, "Just buy any one, and that will tell us which one to buy next." It makes sense, because if we haven't ever owned a microwave, we don't know how we will use it. Therefore, we can't know which special features we will use every day and which ones will prove superfluous. We might ask others to give us their opinions, or even to make the decision for us, or we might struggle to find some way of rationalizing that the model we are about to buy really does make the most sense for us. It is only after we get it home and start to use it, however, that we can come to appreciate what may or may not matter to us. If we use our new microwave just to reheat coffee, for example, we clearly didn't need special buttons for making popcorn or cooking salmon.

There is an important point here: All our decisions are made in ignorance. If we *knew* what to do, we would just do it. That is, we would not be faced with a decision in the first place. The problem is not not knowing; rather, the problem is thinking we should know. Understanding how we approach decisions—and how to make them a vital part of our mindful creativity—is an important part of our personal renaissance. Any new endeavor is rife with decisions we'll have to face without much experience or knowledge. With respect to painting, how can we know what colors we need, in what amounts, and what kinds of brushes we'll want unless we know just what we are going to paint and how we are going to paint it? But if our plan is that exact, the painting is not likely to be created mindfully, nor is it likely to be much fun in the doing.

When faced with a decision, we tend to consider what we think are our options and then predict the consequences we think are likely to result from each. It is in this process that we seem to feel most acutely the difficulty of trying to predict. All of us some of the time, and some of us all the time, become stressed when facing a decision. The more important we believe the outcome will be for us, the harder the decision is to make. Mindful creativity, however, is supposed to be fun; the choices we make in the store today shouldn't weigh heavily on us. Yet these decisions still weigh us down and even keep many of us from proceeding, although our stress is especially foolhardy given the reality of mindful decision making.[1]

The Nature of Decisions

Decision making is relevant to all aspects of our lives, yet most of us move through the day without recognizing the alternatives we have and actively deciding among them. As a result, we give up the feeling of control and mastery that would be ours were we to mindfully create options and then select among them. When we passively move through our day, we set ourselves up to feel like victims. All too often people feel as though they have no choice in situations where others, although no different except in their outlook, actively create their world. It's a powerful advantage to feel in control, especially in the face of entirely new and different situations, where uncertainty is likely to be greatest.

What is the difference between a guess, a prediction, a choice, and a decision? Each characterizes the same process of considering alternatives and selecting one, although a guess deems the affair unimportant, whereas a decision indicates that the outcome is grave. When we are aware that we don't know how to choose or if we don't really care what will happen or if we don't want the responsibility for the outcome, we guess. "I guess I'll take the prize hidden under the box on the left." Consider how odd it would sound if one were to say, "Oh well, I guess I'll get married" or "What the heck, I guess I'll get divorced." Our choice of words also clearly conveys an assessment of confidence in our judgment. Compare "I decided to stop using heroin" to "I guess I'll stop taking heroin." We're often more comfortable "deciding" after the fact and "guessing" before the fact. It may be, then, that the only differences among guesses, predictions, choices, and decisions is the importance we attach to the outcome and the degree of responsibility we're willing to take for it.

Decisions are also hard when we know we don't know yet feel we should know. Any action we are about to take can be seen by us as a guess, a prediction, a choice, or a decision. All concern an unknowable future, but our view of it can indicate very different approaches to that uncertainty. "I'll try these brushes and see how I like them." Better yet, "I'll decide to try these brushes and see how I like them." Better still, "I'll decide to try these brushes and see how I can use them in interesting ways."

It is easier to approach situations as opportunities for mindful decision making when the consequences of the decision do not seem important. As we will learn, however, the importance of our decisions is dependent on how we construe them. If we see only those actions that yield consequences of obvious importance to us as decisions, then we won't see ourselves as having much experience with decision making. The potential consequences for our sense of self for any one decision weigh more heavily if we make only a few decisions a year than if we make numerous decisions every day. We are unlikely to feel competent as decision makers unless we see *many* of our actions as decisions. Engaging our mindful creativity means there are many new decisions to be made. If I have only one chance and I blow it, so to speak, that should create a very different feeling when I head into new situations than if I've recently made twenty decisions and I know I will have twenty more soon to come.

If I fear making the wrong decision, I may seek out others to make it for me and remain oblivious to the fact that I am still making the decision—which is now whether or not to trust the decision just made for me—but I do not reap the benefit of feeling in control for having done so. We make decisions so that we can take action, and our perception of ourselves as good decision makers can be reinforced with each decision we make.

So the more decisions we see ourselves making, the better we feel we are at making decisions. The broader our understanding of what a decision is, especially if we are led to define it for ourselves, the better we feel about making decisions. Most important, people's views of their ability can be influenced by changes in their interpretation of their past actions as decisions, rather than merely reactions to objectively specified alternatives.

Some of us find it easier to make decisions because of a learned tendency to see the bright side. Our evaluations of success or failure, self-efficacy, and contentedness with the outcome of prior decisions all contribute to the ease or difficulty we have with making the next one. But since the generation and evaluation of outcomes is limited only by the motivation of the person to call them to mind for consideration, we can keep generating positive information about our decisions until we have enough to make us feel good about them. Those who have learned to frame information positively may even call up the same information as others, but they consider it from a different perspective, one which suggests the decision was a good one. When I go to a restaurant and the food turns out to be good, I'm pleased. If it turns out not to be to my liking, I eat less, which is also good for me. Thus, my choice of restaurants has worked in my favor whether I liked the food or not. If I instead paid attention to the money I've wasted, I might regret the decision I made and be less confident of my future decision making.

For some people, then, decision making is not stressful at all, because they are content with whatever consequences result. On occasion, when I don't really care whether we go to this restaurant or that, or see one movie instead of another, I choose randomly and offer my choice with confidence. Once our confidence has been established, it may be easier for those who are evaluative to recognize the mindful strength of "it really doesn't matter to me" rather than to see it as weakness. When I was in junior high school, my best friend asked someone else which dress of hers she liked best. I asked her why she didn't request my opinion, and she replied that I would have said I liked all of them. I may not have said that, but she was probably right. I would have liked all of them, each one for a different reason. It became clear to me that I had to develop some dislikes. I chose lima beans. When I'm invited to friends' houses for dinner and they ask if there's anything I don't like, I still confidently state that I like most things but I don't like lima beans. Having this dislike seems to make my likes more believable.

I often decide to give others the chance to make the decision because "the" outcome doesn't matter to me. When they suffer with what they feel is a burden to decide, I randomly, but confidently, make the decision.

Mindful Decision Making

According to most psychologists, decision theorists, economists, and the lay public, our decision making is by nature either rational or irrational. This view essentially leads to the conclusion that to come to a good decision, we should go through a process of assessing costs and benefits, and making our decision based on the result of that calculation.

Despite the prevalence of this view of rational decision making, to make decisions by first doing a cost-benefit analysis brings up the "problem of infinite regress." Before we can make a decision, we need to collect the information required for our calculation. To do so, we need to *decide* on how much information to collect, and then we need to collect information about how much information we should collect to make that decision, and so on. It is a twofold problem. Not only do we not know when to stop collecting information but it may be impossible to obtain reliable information. How do we *decide* what are the costs and what are the benefits to include in our analysis? And if we could specify these, how do we decide on the criteria for our specification, and how do we decide on them, and so on. And, of course, there is the issue of how we decide to decide in the first place. There must be something else at work.

I want to argue that we consider a third, more mindful alternative: Decision making may be neither rational nor irrational but rather arational. The processes that are most generally understood as leading to decisions—such as integrating and weighing information in a cost-benefit analysis—may be post-decision phenomena, if they occur at all, in order to justify our decisions after they are made. Instead of being at the heart of active decision making, the consideration of possible costs typically leads people to passivity.

Let's briefly consider some of the basic premises of this theory before analyzing how we unintentionally rob ourselves of meaningful experience by overlooking this view of decision making. Uncritically accepting our culture's understanding of decision making may play an important part in determining our happiness, and it may be the last barrier between us and our commitment to pursue a creative endeavor.

There are two approaches to making decisions that we need

to distinguish, one active and one passive. Active-deciding, as I define it, differs meaningfully from passive-deciding, which is the approach most people describe when they consider the decision-making process. When we are passive-deciding, we only explore the options we are given and the dimensions these options suggest; we don't generate options for ourselves. As a result, we learn about the world only as it is presented to us. When active-deciding, we take the options presented *and* we explore more alternatives that suggest new dimensions for comparison. We are more likely to come away from active-deciding with a greater knowledge of our options. If we put people back in the equation and realize that the options presented to us are inexactly generated by people, we may be more likely to consider generating our own alternatives. The alternatives we create for ourselves are more likely to meet our needs than are those presented to us. In fact, our research has shown that compared with passive-deciding, active-deciding leads to greater self-esteem, enhanced perceived control, and diminished post-decision regret. Active-deciding is clearly the more mindful and involving of the two processes.[2]

We can now look at a different process of decision making, one that is more mindful and more satisfactory. Whenever we are faced with a decision, we consider our options—they are either psychologically the same or different. If they are psychologically equal, it doesn't make any difference which we choose. If they are not, if one option feels better than the other, there is no decision to make: the positive difference will predetermine our choice. "Objective" differences among the alternatives may lead us to the assumption that there is a meaningful difference between them, but if one alternative does not appear to be better, psychologically they are the same. Do you want option A or option B? If we don't know what each option represents, there is no meaningful difference, so either choice would suffice. If instead we are asked to choose between getting one dollar and getting ten thousand dollars, there isn't really any decision to make.

There is no natural end point to the information we could sensibly consider when making any decision, whether we do so actively or passively. I recently painted a woman wearing formal attire who was putting on lipstick. It wasn't one of my preferred paintings, and I didn't see much of interest in it. I couldn't decide how to make the painting more interesting to me. Even if I had tried to consider all the options open to me, not to mention perform a cost-benefit analysis to figure out which alternative would work best, the process would have been overwhelming. Without regard to such analysis, I just looked closely at what I had already painted and noticed that her rear end was the most dominant aspect of the painting. I "decided" to paint another woman alongside her, back-to-back, with the first woman's rear suggesting an extended stomach for the second. The painting still doesn't have much of a point (although literally it has two), but I like it much better.

Let's consider even a seemingly simple decision such as which surface to paint on. One could consider all the different kinds of surfaces (canvas, Masonite, plywood, oak, birch, a shingle to name just a few), or one could consider the size. One could sensibly consider price, looking at what the various surfaces cost, or what they might cost at another store (and, therefore, which other stores to try before deciding). But it quickly becomes clear that the alternatives seem to be endless even when we try to narrow down the range of options. Decisions in the real world aren't like those in laboratory experiments, where we hold all but a few dimensions constant and lose sight of the fact that there is no natural end point to the amount of information we could sensibly consider. When we passively decide by limiting our options to those presented to us, naturally we similarly hold the world constant, which is fine as long as we remember that we have arbitrarily limited the information we might reasonably have considered if we had let it more naturally vary.

Likewise, there is no natural end point to the number of consequences we could sensibly consider in making a decision. We could consider consequences that seem relevant for today, this week, this year, or posterity. We could consider the consequences of our decision for ourselves now or in the future, for other people we know well, barely know, or may come to know well.

The consequences of our decisions, therefore, have no fixed meaning. Not only can we generate an enormous number of consequences if we want to but the meaning of each consequence may change from different perspectives. If that which is positive is also negative depending on our perspective, how can we decide by calculating the cost and benefit of each potential consequence? They would cancel each other out.

How do we typically make decisions? We gather information until we reach a cognitive commitment, that is, until we come upon a piece of information about which we have a mind-set that leads us to feel, "This is the one." Great, it's on sale; wonderful, this is the last one. I'll take this one because my friend said it was the best. When we first make a cognitive commitment, we freeze the meaning of the information and often unwittingly view it from that frozen perspective in the future. These rigidly held beliefs are not very sensitive to changes in context so that when they are operative, we are unaware of alternative conceptions and we tend to feel the decision process was rational and that, if not the best choice, a good choice was made. In this way, any choice could have been seen as a good choice. When we work backward from the choices we make, it is usually not very hard to find justification for them.

So here may be a more realistic view of how we often make our decisions. We become stressed when we have a decision to make, and if we don't give up at that point of feeling overwhelmed, we try one of several strategies. Sometimes we gather limited information (overlooking just as reasonable alternative information) and then look at the costs and benefits of the consequences we choose to consider, overlooking how costs may be benefits and vice versa. Sometimes we simply make our choice and then relate the process to other people as though we had gone through it before we made our decision rather than after. The mindful alternative is to just feel comfortable arbitrarily making a selection, knowing we can't predict. Instead of worrying about whether we have made the right choice, we make the choice right. We've probably all made decisions in each of these ways on occasion.

There are many shades of green paint available, but I have only enough money with me to buy one tube right now. I arbitrarily buy the one I've never used before, and I make it work. It feels like it was a good decision.

Given that decision making may be reduced to information gathering that ends in a cognitive commitment, people are by nature not better or worse decision makers than others, although they may be more or less likely to have the same cognitive commitments as the person evaluating the decision and, as such, may be deemed to be better or worse at their ability to gather information or be persuasive. If, as I am proposing, there is no complex calculation at work during active or passive decision making, then excluding those people in our culture who are deemed less competent at these complex calculations from important decisions is unjustified.

As important, we can see ourselves as equally good decision makers as others. Every action we take can be construed as a decision. Yet most of us get by just fine for most of the day without weighing the costs and benefits of what we are about to do. Sometimes we don't actively decide because of a mindless lack of an awareness of alternatives. A fruitful strategy would be to generate possible alternatives and consequences for those alternatives, recognizing that there are advantages to each alternative so that any one of them could meet our needs, rendering stress regarding costs and benefits unnecessary.

The illusion of calculated decision making is sustained by our failure to realize the power of uncertainty and the positive consequences of meaning making. We think of uncertainty as a problem to be overcome, and our desire for certainty may be what leads us to accept prepackaged choices rather than deal with an unbounded set of possibilities. Any form of creative engagement almost by definition can encourage us to question the choices we are given: if our choice can be original, then we may see that we can mix and match, so to speak, rather than take the options we are offered. I have no problem not following "the rules" regarding my art. I don't know the rules. If I want to mix a gouache with an acrylic, I will; I have not learned that I shouldn't. The creators of these choices are often not salient, making the options appear etched in stone. As such, they encourage us to accept the status quo. Decision theories assume individuals are motivated to reduce uncertainty, and they may be. If there is no uncertainty, however, the individual is likely to treat that information mindlessly. This is an important point: *Certainty breeds mindlessness. Uncertainty, then, is a friend rather than something to be avoided or feared.*

On the face of it, it seems that we would make better decisions if we were to consider more information, for example, to consider eight pieces of information instead of just four. If one opens up the set of possible relevant pieces of information from multiple perspectives about the options, one's potential preferences in the present and future (considering the myriad ways one may change), the effects that these personal preferences may have on others, and so on, the potential amount of information to be considered is enormous. If this accumulation of data yields even one hundred pieces of information, one may ask whether eight pieces are really more meaningful than just four with respect to the quality of a decision. If it is not, then reducing uncertainty may be a futile goal for decision making.

This is not to say that gathering information is futile. On the contrary, gathering information may be rewarding in its own right, and useful information may surely turn up. Information gathering serves the purposes of differentiating options, finding options, and creating options. The potential utility of this information, however, does not mean that the subsequent decision will be better than it would have been without this information. An alternative would be for the individual to be aware of and accept the fact that decisions involve incomplete information. With an awareness that uncertainty cannot be overcome, the individual may proceed with less stress about making a good decision. Now when I walk into art supply stores I am familiar with many of the paintbrushes others have made available to me. That is satisfying. It is also satisfying to find an unusual (to me) brush, say in a foreign country. It is even more satisfying to take an old brush and cut the bristles in some novel way to create my own brush without knowing exactly how I may come to use it.

If we don't run from it, uncertainty promotes mindfulness. Inasmuch as we confuse the stability of our mind-sets with the stability of the underlying phenomena, there is uncertainty whether we choose to acknowledge it or not. If we make a universal, rather than a personal, attribution for the uncertainty (that is, it is not just that I don't know it but that it is unknowable), then we can be uncertain but still confident.

Taken together, these thoughts and empirical observations suggest that when there is no uncertainty, we give up the opportunity to perceive control in a situation, to learn about new aspects of it, and to meet our current needs to the extent that they may differ from our needs in the past. In short, recognizing the power of uncertainty allows us to grow and promotes a dynamic rather than a static relationship with our world. Thus, we begin any form of creative engagement uncertain of what to do next, what options to consider, or how the option we select will feel to us. That is the reason to pursue it in the first place.[3]

Rather than seeking to reveal a hidden stability within ourselves, the mindful approach to decision making seeks to provide us with a framework in which we may remain open to the processes through which meaning arises within and among people. This openness to the perspective of others and to information viewed as novel allows us to construct meaning. The evaluation of outcomes, which is weighted so heavily in rational choice models, seeks to hold constant both the options and the outcomes involved in a decision without consideration of who put them there. In contrast, mindful decision making emphasizes the experience of control that accompanies a decision to hold neither options nor outcomes stable. When we decide that the determining features of decision making are not either the particular options we select or the particular outcomes we view as preferred, but rather our own freedom to redefine options and reevaluate outcomes as we gather further information, the decision-making process is transformed from either a merely mechanical inevitability (select information until one reaches a cognitive commitment) or a meaningless indeterminacy (select based on a random process because the options are psychologically the same) into an opportunity to exercise personal control.

Thus, there are those who don't worry about making the right decision because they do not think about their predicaments as decisions. There are those who worry about making the right decision because they believe there is a right decision to make. Finally, there are those who don't worry about making the right decision because they realize there is no single right decision to be made. Joining this last group is the final step in removing the roadblocks to mindful creativity and speeding our journey to a personal renaissance.

Epilogue

Where we are is where we've never been.
ELLEN J. LANGER

SO FAR I'VE FOUND THERE ARE THREE GENERAL REWARDS FROM engaging my mindful creativity. First, and perhaps foremost, is the sheer joy the activity brings to me. People can know this only if they engage themselves; it cannot be captured in words. Describing a movie—it was about an adult woman's relationship with her difficult mother—or a three-hour baseball game—it was tied in the bottom of the ninth and then Nomar hit a two-run home run—or summarizing a book one has written or read barely captures the felt experience. To understand, we have to have the experience ourselves. An added benefit is that the felt experience comes, of course with all of the concomitant positive outcomes of being more mindful. Second, the experience is a window to myself. I look at my paintings and ask myself, Why did I paint this at this time? Why a dog now or a person then? Why a serious feeling or a humorous take on something? And why do my views on my views change? I smashed my ankle and was on a medical leave for a semester. It was the beginning of June, graduation time. I painted a woman in cap and gown who, depending on how you look at the painting, is either inside or outside a gate. Did I feel included or excluded? Third, it is a two-way interpersonal mirror. Why do some people like this one and not that one and others the reverse? Why am I willing to show my paintings to some people and not others? Who do I trust and why? Perhaps I should either change those distrustful relationships or remove them from my life. Life is too short to admit impediments. And thus my mindful creativity plays the part of helping me grow.

At first I painted to see if I could do it. I shared my paintings with friends and then took a bigger leap in going public. I am represented by one of Provincetown's finest galleries, The Julie Heller Gallery, and more recently by J & W Gallery in New Hope, Pennsylvania. Strangers to me see my work in a situation where I cannot make excuses or tell them of my other life. The paintings are whatever they are on their own. For better or worse, people have said that I have my own style. Anthony took it further and asked, Now that you've created a vocabulary, what do you want to say with it? I said, I'm not sure. I'm ready for the next step, but as with all next steps, I won't be able to describe it until I've already done it. What I do know is that I'm now free from many constraints that bound me. Unencumbered by fear of evaluation, my mindful creativity can continue to nurture my ongoing personal renaissance.

I believe that our natural, mindful creativity should be the way we experience most, if not all, of our days. By engaging in some new activity—whether it is art, music, sports, gardening, or cooking—on an ongoing basis, we can begin to experience what it is like to be more mindful. Most of the time mindlessness comes by default, not by design, and when we are mindless we're oblivious to being so. We need to find a way to cue us into our mindlessness. We need a bell that will sound for us, signaling that we are acting mindlessly. When we let ourselves fully engage a new task and see how exciting it feels, as soon as we feel otherwise the bell should sound. If we remove the roadblocks, we can begin to engage ourselves, again.

And so, by removing the roadblocks we've discussed, it will be easier to begin to live more mindfully. All of these roadblocks are related to one another, so removing even one or two may have a cascading effect. Comparing ourselves with others to see if we are better or worse at something than they are, for example, would make no sense if we reevaluated evaluation. Mistakes and fixed ideas about talent similarly should change in meaning. Once we recognize that these evaluations were put in place by people whose intentions and motivations are not stable across context, absolute evaluations give way to either a nonevaluative outlook or, at least, an understanding that evaluations depend on context for their meaning. Once we mindfully engage something that we might not have liked initially and see how our feelings about it change, we are more likely to question the idea of fixed evaluations. The more we do to remove any of these roadblocks, the more we should be led to question the others. Thus, the more we engage our mindful creativity, the closer we may get to living a mindful life. By living a life full of art, we may achieve an artful life.

Mindful Creativity and a Mindful Life

*In the perspective of every person lies a lens through which
we may better understand ourselves.*
ELLEN J. LANGER

Let me end essentially where I began, with my own story. Before I started to paint, I had begun what eventually would become this book. I had many ideas that were meaningful to me, numerous observations of human behavior and experiments to help clarify those ideas. The question I struggled with was how to present these ideas. It was like having a closet floor full of clothes in need of hangers. My art provided a way to get the clothes off the floor, so to speak. More important, however, than just a way to structure the book, my art enabled me to test personally the ideas I believe help promote more mindful living. I am suggesting that engaging in a creative activity can promote greater mindfulness in all of our endeavors. Paint for fun, paint for a richer life. I am not suggesting that anyone needs to show her or his work or take a "public" path. I had anything but reason to think that painting would provide the joy it has for me. By putting myself out there once I started, however, I would experience firsthand the angst, fears, and embarrassment this book tries to eliminate. If I could not do it, I could not write about it.

People feel they are the masters of their fate, but much of the time, as years of social psychological research has shown, we are instead products of the circumstances in which we find ourselves. We behave in ways that are based on the mind-sets we have about the situations in which we find ourselves, rather than as a function of who we think we are. Thus, whether we help someone in distress, obey authority, compete, conform, or simply enjoy ourselves is a result of the situation we encounter. This is why social psychologists can show us that we have multiple selves. We do not, however, all behave the same way in any situation. We have different, mindless understandings of the "situation," and these different constructs lead us to different behavior. The fact that we don't all behave the same way suggests that we could have choices we are not aware of in any of these situations—even those where we feel locked in. The roadblocks that prevent our mindful creativity are examples of some of these mindless situational understandings. Once we remove them and experience our authentic selves, we may actually become the masters of our fate.

Notes

1. A Life of Mindful Creativity

1. Arie Kruglanski and Donna Webster have shown that much of empirical evidence in cognitive and social psychology points to parallel motivations to "seize" on particular rules, principles, and cognitive frames, then prematurely "freeze" them in place, even after they have become counterproductive. See A. Kruglanski and D. Webster, "Motivated Closing of the Mind: Seizing and Freezing," *Psychological Review,* April 1996.

2. Unfortunately, we are laboring under a Platonic tradition grounded in the belief that there exists an ultimate, non-contingent theory that can explain all facts seamlessly (see I. Berlin, *The Proper Study of Mankind,* Oxford: Oxford University Press, 1997) and under a neo-Kantian tradition in cognitive psychology that bids us look for contingency-free "a priori" structures that can be used to explain unconditionally all facts about human mental processes.

3. Besides, many of the authors arguing for the structuration of thinking into routines seem to believe that thinking in itself is valuable only as a means to the end we are thinking toward. The *process* of getting there matters far less than the end result. Indeed classical decision theory labors under the utilitarian

heritage of the Anglo-American tradition inspired by the original utilitarian arguments of J. Bentham and J. S. Mill.

2. Becoming Authentic

1. And classics of Western literature like Proust's *Remembrance of Things Past* and Joyce's *Ulysses* found their monumental journeys inward on vividly felt (but otherwise "mundane" or "everyday") experiences. Of course, it is their "everydayness" that makes experiencing them creatively so striking.

2. E. Langer and J. Sviokla, "Charisma from a Mindfulness Perspective," unpublished manuscript, Harvard University, 1988. See also *Mindfulness:* 147–48.

3. Ibid.

4. C. Kawakami, J. White, and E. J. Langer, "Mindful and Masculine: Freeing Female Leaders from Gender Role Constraints," *Journal of Social Issues* 56 (2000): 49–64.

5. R. J. Burke and G. MacDermid, "Gender Awareness Education in Organizations," *Psychological Reports* 79 (1996): 1071–74.

6. E. Langer and J. Preston, "The Individuating Effects of Mindfulness: Avoiding Stereotyping," unpublished manuscript, Harvard, 2002.

7. M. Hussain and E. Langer, "A Cost of Pretending," *Journal of Adult Development* 10, no. 4 (2003): 261–70.

8. E. Langer, A. Filipowicz, T. Russell, N. Eisenkraft, and N. Sommaripa, "The Visibility of Mindfulness: Mindful versus Mindless Art," manuscript in prep., Harvard University, 2002.

9. Ibid.

10. Traditional approaches to the representation of how people make decisions or render judgments (see, for instance, D.

Kreps, *Notes on the Theory of Choice,* Boulder, Colo.: Westview Press, 1989) do not typically incorporate a preference for novelty or for being surprised by the outcome of a predicament. It is not hard to understand why: the analytical apparatus of decision theory is confined to speaking of well-determined and definable events and event types, whereas "the unknown" is difficult to capture in a mathematical formalism.

3. The Tyranny of Evaluation

1. Michel Foucault persuasively argued that people internalize and make real for themselves rules, sanctions, and restrictions forcefully imposed on them from the outside. In *Discipline and Punish,* a history of the birth of the modern prison, he describes an architectural device (the panopticon) that allows prison guards to monitor their prisoners at all times *without* the prisoners' explicit awareness that they are being monitored. In the face of ubiquitous, random, and undetectable monitoring, regulation of prisoners' behavior turned into self-regulation. In subsequent writings, Foucault extended the notion of the panopticon to an analysis of social order itself, highlighting the means by which we internalize processes of external evaluation.

2. We have, during the past century, been living under Nietzsche's admonition that it is at once possible and desirable to attempt a "re-valuation of all values" (see *Beyond Good and Evil,* 1884; New York: Dover, 1986), and twentieth-century Western philosophy has offered some cursory glimpses through the thick cover of naïve realism about the value of objects and events, but old habits are resilient to counterarguments.

3. S. Snow and E. Langer, unpublished data, Harvard University. See also *The Power of Mindful Learning:* 58–59.

4. Indeed, the current "crisis" in the explanatory project of the natural sciences and the legitimacy of scientific institutions comes not so much from a natural "end of science" because it has run out of subjects but rather from a newfound awareness in the public sphere of the many possible standards by which discourse can be evaluated. Multiple, incommensurable ways of being and talking had always existed, but post-Kuhn, we have become increasingly aware of their existence and incommensurability (see T. Kuhn, *The Structure of Scientific Revolutions,* Chicago: University of Chicago Press, 1962; T. Kuhn, *The Road Since Structure,* Cambridge, Mass.: MIT Press, 1990).

5. See E. Jones and R. Nisbett, "The Actor and the Observer: Divergent Perceptions of the Causes of Behavior," in *Attributions: Perceiving the Causes of Behavior,* ed. E. Jones et al. (Morristown, N.J.: General Learning Press, 1972).

6. L. Ross, D. Greene, and P. House, "The False Consensus Effect: An Egocentric Bias in Social Perception and Attribution Processes," *Journal of Experimental Social Psychology* 13 (1977): 279–301.

7. M. Storms, "Videotape and the Attribution Process: Reversing Actors' and Observers' Points of View," *Journal of Personality and Social Psychology* 27 (1973): 165–75.

8. S. M. Popp, "Alcohol Use and Occupational Culture in the Skilled Building Trades: An Ethnographic Study," *Dissertation Abstracts International* 57 (12, 1997): 5203-A.

9. R. Fazio, E. Effrein, and V. Falender, "Self-Perceptions Following Social Interaction," *Journal of Personality and Social Psychology* 41 (2), (1981): 232–42.

10. D. Adlow, "Young New England Paintings," *Magazine of Art,* May 1938, 293.

11. Indeed, logical analysis of the history of science (or what we call philosophy of science) reveals that the scientist—reputed

purveyor of "objective truths"—constantly makes choices that are more or less arbitrary: about what theory to test, about what apparatus to build in order to test it, about which predictions to include in early experimental tests of the theory, about which observations to allow as truly "validating" or "invalidating" of the theory, about when to discard a theory that has been "invalidated," and so forth (see I. Lakatos, "Falsification and the Methodology of Scientific Research Programmes," in *Criticism and the Growth of Knowledge,* eds. I. Lakatos and A. Musgrave, Cambridge: Cambridge University Press, 1970). Of course, after all these "choices," the theories in question find their ways into textbooks, where they are presented in the form of timeless truths.

12. *New York Times,* "In a Weird Way, David Lynch Makes Sense," March 10, 2002, 22. Many twentieth-century phenomenologists, such as Martin Heidegger and Henri Bergson, draw our attention to the fact that "thoughts come to us, not we to them."

13. Langer, Lee, and Yariv, unpublished data, Harvard University, 2000.

14. E. Langer, I. Janis, and J. A. Wolfer, "Reduction of Psychological Stress in Surgical Patients," *Journal of Experimental Social Psychology* 11 (1975): 155–65.

4. The Mindfulness of Mistakes

1. Mistakes—or failed predictions and explanations—have been hailed as the cornerstones of progress in both laboratory science and action science. In his *Logic of Scientific Discovery* (London: Hutchinson, 1959), Karl Popper articulated a logic of scientific progress whereby "better" theories are those that, given more opportunity to err, ended up erring less than others. Giving a theory the opportunity to err (rather than shielding it from "mistakes") is also crucial to Chris Argyris's

logic of "action science" (see C. Argyris, *On Organizational Learning*, Cambridge, Mass.: Harvard University Press, 1993), which aims to uncover defensive routines and strategies of people trying to protect their theories from error.

2. Rosamond Bernier, *Matisse, Picasso, Miró: As I Knew Them* (New York: Alfred A. Knopf, 1991): 272. In his monograph on the psychological correlates of genius, Hans Eysenck schematized his conception of a genius as a "random number generator coupled to a good filter." Most people focus on "the good filter," but it is quite often the "random number generator" that we need the most help producing, as truly random behavior is truly difficult to come by (especially purposefully). Hence, it made perfect sense for Miró to allow a truly random pattern to start him off thinking about the subject and execution of his next painting (see H. Eysenck, *Genius*, Cambridge: Cambridge University Press, 1995).

3. E. Langer, Y. Steshenko, B. Cummings, N. Eisenkraft, and S. Campbell, "Mistakes as a Mindful Cue," prepublication manuscript, Harvard University, 2004.

4. And there is no reason to believe that, in some future, no matter how distant, there *will* be a set of rules that are fail-safe, in the sense that they can be used to prove their own validity. The rules of logic themselves cannot be used to prove that logic is valid (by its own standards), as the philosopher Hilary Putnam showed on the basis of his insightful interpretation of the famed "Gödel Theorem" establishing the incompleteness of formal systems with at least the complexity of arithmetic (see T. Nagel and E. Newman, *Gödel's Proof*, New York: Dover, 1958).

5. R. Feynman, *Lectures on Physics* (Reading, Mass.: Addison-Wesley, 1989).

6. J. S. Bruner and M. C. Potter, "Interference in Visual Recognition," *Science* 144 (1964): 424–25.

7. And it is this uncertainty—about the "what" of what will come next—that has been identified as a sign of "ontological insecurity" typical of psychologically pathological individuals. However, scientific reasoning itself—that presumed safe haven from "irrationality," is fundamentally ambiguous regarding the objects that populate its theories. And we have, in our classical twentieth-century repertoire, very little idea about how to resolve ontological uncertainty (for a discussion see Brian Cantwell Smith, *The Origin of Objects,* Cambridge, Mass.: MIT Press, 1995).

8. R. Frost, "The Figure a Poem Makes," in *Best American Essays of the Century,* eds. J. Oates and R. Atwan (Boston: Houghton Mifflin, 1991).

5. The Rule of Absolutes

1. M. Battin, J. Fisher, R. Moore, and A. Silvers, *Puzzles About Art* (Boston and New York: St. Martin's Press, Bedford Books, 1989).

2. As pointed out in Chapter 4, there are very good reasons to assume that "the" set of rules by which to govern our minds will never be found—not because it is unreachable but because it is a chimera—provably so, thanks to Kurt Gödel's work. Ever prescient, Friedrich Nietzsche intuited this result a full fifty years earlier: "This is my way"—says his Zarathustra. "Where is *your* way? *The* way—that does not exist." (See Friedrich Nietzsche, *Thus Spoke Zarathustra,* New York: Penguin Books, 1978.)

3. I. Dror and E. Langer, "The Danger of Knowing Too Much: Cognition Plasticity and Knowledge," unpublished manuscript, Harvard University, 2001.

4. E. Langer and A. Grant, "Putting Subjectivity Back in the

Equation," prepublication manuscript, Harvard University, 2004.

5. M. E. Seligman, *Helplessness: On Development, Depression and Death* (San Francisco: Freeman, 1975).

6. Langer and Grant, "Putting Subjectivity Back in the Equation."

7. L. D. Ross, T. M. Amabile, and J. L. Steinmetz, "Social Roles, Social Control, and Biases in Social Perception Processes," *Journal of Personality and Social Psychology* 35 (1977): 485–94.

8. Psychology has labored for the past fifty years under a very narrow, computational definition of intelligence, grounded in the "mind-as-computer" metaphor, as Dan Goldstein and Gerd Gigerenzer have put it ("Mind As Computer: The Birth of a Metaphor," *Journal of Creativity Research,* 9 (1996): 131–44). By that definition, a "more" intelligent person is "more" like a computer in his or her cognitive processes. Fortunately, there has been a recent resurgence of investigations of intelligence that are not computational—and that stress the highly ingenious ways humans deal with complex predicaments through both the creation *and* the reduction of uncertainty and ambiguity.

9. George Dickie, *Art and the Aesthetic: An Institutional Analysis* (Ithaca: Cornell University Press, 1974).

10. W. Smith and E. Langer, "The Art of Engagement—The Engagement of Art," prepublication manuscript, Harvard University, 2004.

6. The Mindlessness of Social Comparison

1. P. Lockwood and Z. Kunda, "Superstars and Me: Predicting the Impact of Role Models on the Self," *Journal of Personality and Social Psychology* 73 (1997): 91–103.

2. M. D. Alicke, F. M. LoSchiavo, J. I. Zerbst, and S. Zhang, "The Person Who Outperforms Me Is a Genius: Esteem Maintenance in Upward Social Comparison," *Journal of Personality and Social Psychology* 73 (1997): 781–89.

3. L. Festinger, "A Theory of Social Comparison Processes," *Human Relations* 7 (1954): 117–40.

4. E. Langer and L. Imber, "The Role of Mindlessness in the Perception of Deviance," *Journal of Personality and Social Psychology* 39 (1980): 360–67. Also, E. Langer, *Mindfulness* (Reading, Mass.: Addison-Wesley, 1989).

5. J. White, E. Langer, L. Yariv, and J. Welch, "The Negative Effects of Social Comparison," *Journal of Adult Development.* In press.

6. D. Hockney, *Secret Knowledge: Rediscovering the Lost Techniques of the Old Masters* (New York: Viking Press, 2001).

7. *New York Times,* November 25, 2001: 34.

8. Nineteenth- and early-twentieth-century artists were often schooled in the famous *Cours de Dessin* by the famous French art pedagogue Charles Bargh, which aimed to break drawing into a simple—and simply masterable—set of mechanical and coordinative skills. The course is based on having the student first trace and then copy master prints and drawings of past artists, with the aim of producing precise replicas. This kind of education is now making a comeback in "representational" art circles as a way of producing artists who are more competent at representing three-dimensional forms, but the twenty-first century owes it to its origins to produce a new *Cours de Dessin,* based on mastering rendering the ineffable through subtle distortions rather than through exact replication. No such *Cours* is currently available.

9. S. Schachter, *The Psychology of Affiliation* (Stanford, Calif.: Stanford University Press, 1959).

10. D. Frable, T. Blackstone, and C. Scherbaum, "Marginal and Mindful: Deviance in Social Interactions," *Journal of Personality and Social Psychology* 59 (1990): 140–49.

11. For more information, see www.elephantart.com.

12. But, of course, we may be all confused about what others think about us most of the time. As Ray Nickerson has shown ("How-We Know—and Sometimes Misjudge—What Others Know: Imputing One's Own Knowledge to Others," *Psychological Bulletin* 125 (1999): 737–59), people more often than not misjudge what others think, or what others think they think, even as they gleefully base their actions and subsequent thoughts on these false assumptions.

13. W. B. Swann, Jr., B. W. Pelham, and D. S. Krull, "Agreeable Fancy or Disagreeable Truth? How People Reconcile Their Self-Enhancement and Self-Verification Needs," *Journal of Personality and Social Psychology* 57 (1989): 782–91.

14. A. Tessor and J. Smith, "Some Effects of Task Relevance and Friendship on Helping: You Don't Always Help the One You Like," *Journal of Experimental Social Psychology* 16 (1980): 582–90.

7. The Myth of Talent

1. Ericsson, Krampe, and Tesch-Romer ("The Role of Deliberate Practice in the Acquisition of Expert Performance," *Psychological Review* 100, 1993): 363–406) have shown that what we normally attribute to "genius" or unusual talent in artists is often the result of a minimum of ten years of patient, dedicated work.

2. In his study of genius by the same name (Cambridge: Cambridge University Press, 1995), Hans Eysenck has persuasively shown that most of the causal connections we make with

"genius" performance (relating genius to genetic inheritance, cultural factors, upbringing, and so forth) are illusory: For every causal covering law relating a variable outside of our control to "genius" there are sufficient exceptions to place the covering law in doubt.

3. M. Blume, *A French Affair: The Paris Beat,* 1965–1998 (New York: Plume Books, 2000).

4. P. Brook, *International Herald Tribune,* March 9, 1996.

5. W. Heisenberg, *Physics and Beyond* (London: Allen & Unwin, 1971).

6. P. L. Carlen, G. Wortzman, R. C. Holgate, D. A. Wilkerson, and R. G. Rankin, "Reversible Cerebral Atrophy in Recently Abstinent Chronic Alcoholics Measured by Computed Tomography Scans," *Science* 200 (1978): 1076–78. In the past we believed that all brain damage is irreversible. Now we believe some is reversible. In my view, we will find support over time that all brain damage is reversible.

7. R. Janoff-Bulman and P. Brickman, "Expectations and What People Learn from Failure," in *Expectations and Actions: Expectancy-Value Models in Psychology,* ed. N. Feather (Hillsdale, N.J.: Lawrence Erlbaum, 1982). Also see C. B. Wortman and J. W. Brehm, "Responses to Uncontrollable Outcomes: An Integration of Reactance Theory and the Learned Helplessness Model," in *Advances in Experimental Social Psychology,* 8, ed. L. Berkowitz (New York: Academic Press, 1975).

8. N. T. Feather, "Attribution of Responsibility and Valence of Success and Failure in Relation to Initial Confidence and Task Performance," *Journal of Personality and Social Psychology* 13 (1969): 129–142 and B. Weiner, *Theories of Motivation: From Mechanism to Cognition* (Chicago: Markham, 1972).

9. E. Langer, J. Johnson, and H. Botwinick, "Nothing Succeeds Like Success, Except . . . ," in *The Psychology of Control*, ed. F. Langer (Los Angeles: Sage Publications, 1983).

10. Ibid.

11. As Friedrich Nietzsche himself—the demolition artist in the realm of values and metaphysics—admonished in his *Beyond Good and Evil* (1884).

8. The Blindness of Knowing

1. R. S. Nickerson and M. J. Adams, "Long-Term Memory for a Common Object," *Cognitive Psychology* 11 (1979): 287–307.

2. D. J. Simons and D. T. Levin, "Failure to Detect Changes to People During a Real-World Interaction," *Psychonomic Bulletin and Review* 5 (1998): 644–49.

3. J. S. Bruner and M. C. Potter, "Interference in Visual Recognition," *Science* 144 (1964): 424–25.

4. E. Loftus, *Eyewitness Testimony*, rev. ed. (Cambridge, Mass.: Harvard University Press, 1996).

9. From Reference to Preference

1. G. Stein, *Paris France: Personal Recollections* (New York: Charles Scribner's Sons, 1940).

2. S. Long, "The Effects of Mindfulness of Brand Preference and Eating," unpublished manuscript, Harvard University, 2002.

3. A. Marcus and E. Langer, "Mindfulness as a Means of Reducing Conformity," unpublished manuscript, Harvard University, 1990.

4. E. Langer, S. Taylor, S. Fiske, and B. Chanowitz, "Stigma, Staring and Discomfort: A Novel Stimulus Hypothesis," *Journal of Experimental Social Psychology* 12 (1976): 451–63.

5. E. Langer and L. Imber, "The Role of Mindlessness in the Perception of Deviance," *Journal of Personality and Social Psychology* 39 (1980): 360–67.

6. E. Langer, R. Bashner, and B. Chanowitz, "Decreasing Prejudice by Increasing Discrimination," *Journal of Personality and Social Psychology* 49 (1985): 1–8.

7. S. Golub, M. Kozak, and E. Langer, "Reducing Prejudice Through Mindful Distinction Drawing," unpublished manuscript, Harvard University, 2004.

8. L. Coates-Burpee and E. Langer, "Mindfulness and Marital Satisfaction," *Journal of Adult Development*, in press.

9. Philip Goldberg, "Are Women Prejudiced Against Women?" *Transaction*, April 1969.

10. W. Smith and E. Langer, "The Art of Engagement: The Engagement of Art," unpublished manuscript, Harvard University, 2004.

11. See *Mindfulness* for a review of this research.

10. The Mindful Choice

1. See "The Illusion of Calculated Decision Making," in *Beliefs, Reasoning, and Decision Making*, eds. R. Shank and E. Langer (Mahwah, N.J.: Lawrence Erlbaum Associates, 1994).

2. E. Langer, "The Illusion of Control," *Journal of Personality and Social Psychology* 32 (1975): 311–28.

3. Choices may have important consequences, but that does not

mean our decision was good or bad. And there is no natural end point to the number of consequences we could consider. Furthermore, for the last time, each consequence may be simultaneously good or bad or neutral, depending on the perspective from which we view it.

Index

About the Author

ELLEN J. LANGER is the author of two bestselling books: *Mindfulness,* which has sold more than 150,000 copies in thirteen languages, and *The Power of Mindful Learning.* Langer is a professor of psychology at Harvard University. Dr. Langer is the recipient of, among numerous awards and honors, a Guggenheim Fellowship, the Award for Distinguished Contributions to Psychology in the Public Interest from the American Psychological Association, and the Award for Distinguished Contributions of Basic Science to the Application of Psychology.